GCSE English

for AQA A

Imelda Pilgrim   Consultant: Peter Buckroyd

Experienced examiners

Heinemann Educational Publishers
Halley Court, Jordan Hill, Oxford OX2 8EJ
a division of Reed Educational & Professional Publishing Ltd

Heinemann is a registered trademark of Reed Educational & Professional Publishing Ltd

OXFORD   MELBOURNE   AUCKLAND
JOHANNESBURG   BLANTYRE   GABORONE
IBADAN   PORTSMOUTH NH (USA)   CHICAGO

© Imelda Pilgrim 2002

Consultant: Peter Buckroyd

First published in 2002
07   06   05   04   03   02
10 9 8 7 6 5 4 3 2 1

British Library Cataloguing in Publication Data is available from the
British Library on request.

ISBN 0 435 10602 3

Dedication
For lovely Beth

Thanks to Marian Slee, Mike Hamlin and the English department at Acklam Grange School for their help.

Special thanks to Lindsay McNab for his contribution.

Edited by Jane Robertson

Designed and produced by Gecko Ltd, Bicester, Oxon

Cover design by hicksdesign

Cover image by Photodisc

Original illustrations © Heinemann Educational Publishers 2002

Illustrated by James Brown, Alice Englander, Julian Mosedale, Jennifer Ward, Jonathan Williams, DTP Gecko

Printed and bound in the UK by Bath Colour Books

Tel: 01865 888058 www.heinemann.co.uk

Many students ask how they can prepare for GCSE English. Other subjects have content to revise so that you can be clear about exactly what you need to know. GCSE English assesses the reading and writing skills you have been developing for most of your life. So how can you improve these skills for your examination?

The good news is that there *are* specific things you can do to improve your skills in English and make sure you are fully prepared for the examination. You can find out and really understand exactly what each paper will test. Then you can make sure you have practised reading and responding to the sorts of texts you will find on the exam papers. Finally, you can experiment with, and develop, a range of writing styles to enable you to write in a fluent and interesting way.

GCSE English for AQA A ensures you cover exactly what is needed for each examination paper:

Paper 1:	*Section A*	Reading response to non-fiction and media texts
	Section B	Writing to argue, persuade or advise
Paper 2:	*Section A*	Reading response to poems from different cultures and traditions in the **AQA A Anthology**
	Section B	Writing to inform, explain or describe.

This book is designed to help you do as well as you possibly can in these papers. We hope you enjoy working with the variety of texts and activities that you find in it and that you are successful in your final examination.

About the author

Imelda Pilgrim is a practising English teacher and an experienced examiner for GCSE English.

CONTENTS

PAPER 2

HOW TO USE THIS BOOK

This book takes you through each element of your GCSE English examinations. You may find it easiest to work through the sections in the order they appear, although this is not essential.

As you progress through this book you will:

- learn about the specific skills you will be tested on in each of the English papers
- find a wide range of texts and activities designed to help you improve these skills
- work through examples of different kinds of examination questions
- learn how to plan and develop your answers.

There are also specimen examination papers for you to try, once you have worked through the appropriate sections. Your teacher will tell you whether you should use the Foundation or Higher Tier papers.

This symbol indicates whther a table can be downloaded from the web. Go to www.heinemann.co.uk/usersupport and enter your password aqaasuccess

You have spent nearly all your life developing your skills in English, from infancy when you started to use language in speech, through those early experiences in reading and writing, when you struggled to make sense of simple words in a child's text and to write those same words in a clear form. As a young child, your skills in English developed rapidly. Before long you were reading whole texts and writing poems, short stories, diaries and letters of your own.

During Key Stage 3 you will have read a wider range of texts and become more aware of their complexities. In writing, you will have developed a more sophisticated range of vocabulary and sentence structures and learned new ways to organise your ideas. Now you are preparing for your GCSE examinations in English. You need to consolidate the skills you have, develop new ones and learn how to use these to your best advantage.

Although reading and writing are assessed separately in the English examinations, they are very closely linked. You will find, therefore, that the work you do on reading often has implications for your writing, and vice versa.

Developing your reading skills

In addition to working through this book, one of the best ways you can help yourself is by doing as much reading as you can. The GCSE years are busy ones and it is easy to neglect private reading. Nevertheless, it is by reading widely that you will develop an understanding of how texts are organised and of how language can be used to achieve maximum impact. You will also learn new vocabulary, new sentence structures and new ways of organising ideas, all of which will help you in your writing. Aim for variety and set some time aside every day for reading.

Take more notice of the reading materials all around you. Start to read leaflets, newsletters, magazine and newspaper articles and adverts more critically. Think about how they match what you are learning about presentation and content. Are they effective? If so, why? The more thought you give to the reading materials that surround you, the more you will understand how you are influenced by them.

Developing your writing skills

Every piece of writing you do, whether it be a diary entry, a letter, notes or an imaginative story, has a specific purpose and audience – a reason for writing and an intended reader. As you are writing it is important that you keep both your purpose and audience in mind so that what you write is both relevant and appropriate.

Aim to develop your awareness of how you and other people write. Think about the way sentences are constructed. Look at the way words are used to create a particular effect and start to expand your range of words. Above all, don't be afraid to experiment with new ideas and new methods. By doing so, you will find that the quality of your writing improves and that the experience of writing becomes altogether more challenging, exciting and rewarding.

Paper 1

This paper examines **Reading** in Section A and **Writing** in Section B. Each section is worth 15% of your final mark for English.

Paper 1 (1 hour 45 minutes)

Section A requires reading responses to unseen non-fiction and media texts.

Section B requires one piece of writing which argues, persuades or advises, linked to theme(s) or topic(s) of the stimulus materials in Section A. Candidates will be offered a choice of questions.

Section A: *Reading Response to Non-Fiction and Media Texts*

An examiner uses a mark scheme to assess your work. This mark scheme is based on certain Assessment Objectives. The Assessment Objectives for reading in Paper 1 Section A focus on five main areas:

- distinguish between fact and opinion
- follow an argument
- understand and evaluate how writers use linguistic, structural and presentational devices
- select and collate material according to purpose
- read with insight and engagement.

The following pages take you through these **five** areas, explaining what skills you need and providing examples and activities to help you develop them.

1 Exploring fact and opinion

A *fact* is something which can be proved to be true:

The moon is the earth's only natural satellite.

You might know this already or you could check it in an encyclopaedia or on the internet.

A *false fact* is something which can be proved to be untrue:

The moon is only 100 miles away.

This would also be easy to check, although you would probably realise it was incorrect.

An *opinion* is a point of view which cannot be proved to be true or untrue:

It would be brilliant to live on the moon.

It might be, but then again it might create dreadful pollution and other problems.

Notice how an opinion can be stated as though it were a fact.

Activity 1

Read the following statements and sort them into *facts*, *false facts* and *opinions*.

Write the number of the statement and F, FF or O next to it.

1 The American astronaut, Buzz Lightyear, was the first person to walk on the moon.
2 Man's landing on the moon is the greatest achievement of the twentieth century.
3 The gravitational attraction of the moon causes tides to rise and fall in the earth's oceans.
4 A man first walked on the moon in July 1969.
5 The position of the moon directly affects your star sign.
6 The word 'lunar' originates from the Latin word 'luna', meaning the moon.
7 The letters NASA stand for National Aeronautics and Space Administration.
8 In the nursery rhyme 'Hey diddle diddle', the cat jumped over the moon.

Now discuss with a partner:

• how you made your decisions   • how you could check your choices.

Sometimes it is not too difficult to tell the difference between *fact, false fact* and *opinion*. At other times you have to read very carefully to distinguish one from the other.

Check the facts: surveys

Something may be a 'fact' but may be based on very little evidence, or evidence that is misleading. For example:

1 **A survey of cat owners may show that 90% of them use a particular brand of cat food.**

   What difference would it make to this 'fact' if the survey was done next to the supermarket shelves selling that particular brand?

2 **A survey of parents may show that 74% of them are happy with the nursery provision for children.**

   To what extent do the results of this survey depend on the area where it was carried out?

Identifying opinions

Not all surveys are unreliable. A recent survey, following the publication of GCSE results, showed that 57.1% of pupils gained a grade C or above in their GCSE exams across all subjects. This is a fairly reliable figure as it takes into account all the candidates sitting GCSEs in a particular year. Even so, this information may then be presented in very different ways, as shown in the following newspaper headlines.

Read them closely and identify:

- the fact that is used in both
- the different opinions
- an example of an opinion being expressed as a fact
- which creates a positive and which creates a negative impression.

Our children are getting cleverer and the facts prove it
Recent figures show that more children than ever are achieving grade C in their GCSE exams.

EXAMS GET EASIER AS MORE CHILDREN ACHIEVE GRADE C OR ABOVE

Neither of these newspapers could prove their claims. The writers are allowing their feelings to influence their judgements; they are showing bias. Bias is often shown in people's opinions and, as you have seen above, can seem to be based on facts. The bias is created by:

- the way the facts are selected
- the way the facts are used.

You can find out more about bias on page 23.

Write your own positive and negative headlines for a survey that has found:

Over two-thirds of all teenagers think they will get married but only half of these believe marriage should be for ever.

You do not need to include all the information in each headline.

As you read the following newspaper editorial, list the use of:

• facts
• opinions
• evidence used to support opinion or fact.

The first paragraph has been annotated already. Notice how a sentence can contain a mixture of fact and opinion.

More about opinions: editorials

Most newspapers carry an editorial comment or leader linked to an item that is currently in the news. This is generally an expression of opinion by the editor, designed to influence the thinking of the reader.

Air guns must be banned

opinion ────

opinion ────

opinion ────

opinion ────

It is shocking to learn that as many as half of the guns now found at crime scenes are air pistols, which can be easily obtained over the counter. As our reporter discovered, these pistols, which bear a striking
5   resemblance to real guns, are cheap, readily available and can be converted within hours to carry live ammunition.

──── fact

──── evidence

──── opinion

──── fact

These guns are not just being used as threats. They are already taking innocent lives. Last October a Bradford taxi driver was shot dead in an air gun attack and just a
10 few days ago a London woman was shot in the stomach. Horrific experiences such as these will be prevented only if the sale of air guns is banned.

Isn't it time David Blunkett heeded the advice of experienced police officers and closed the legal loophole
15 which allows widespread abuse of these guns?

The Dunblane massacre is a sorry reminder of how much suffering can be caused when weapons are allowed to fall into the wrong hands.

The Government was right to respond to that tragedy
20 by implementing a new law to ban handguns. It should apply the same logic now and find a way of putting these life-threatening pistols out of harm's way.

Daily Express

How words can reinforce opinion

Words can be used to influence the reader and reinforce an opinion, particularly in advertising or promotional material. Read the following advertisement closely.

Changing your hair colour should be easy. But, by the time you've read through the
5 confusing instructions for most home hair colourants, you're often left with just two choices – chance it and
10 risk disappointment or forget it and carry on dreaming about that ideal hair colour.

You need dream no more. Hair colour experts Alberto VO5 have made hair colouring easy with new VO5 Select. Its unique VO5 Select Indicator
15 makes it easy to choose a colour. On one side of the pack you'll find the shade close to your natural colour and on the other, a guide to the expected colour result – it's that simple.

The new VO5 Select range comprises 12
20 fantastic wash-in, wash-out colours, which last up to eight washes and contain no ammonia or peroxide. It is the first semi-permanent range to include vibrant fashion shades as well as natural shades to cover grey, and the first to be
25 awarded the Plain English Campaign's coveted Crystal Mark for its clear instructions. Each box, costing just £5.25, contains a sealing rinse to condition, protect and reduce colour fading – so your hair will always look its shiny best.
30 What about application? VO5 Select's specially designed cap reduces any messy drips, and speeds up the colour development time using the heat from your head. Such a simple approach and a unique money-back guarantee
35 means it's the ideal choice for first-time colourers. In fact, it's perfect for anyone who wants beautifully coloured hair with no fuss!

Activity 4

1 Make a list of the phrases in the advertisement that suggest the product is easy to use. You should find at least eight.

2 Copy and complete the following chart to identify and explain the opinion being suggested by the words in **bold**. The first one is done for you, with the explanation in short note form as well. You can use this note form if you prefer.

What the words actually say (denotation)	What the words suggest (connotation)
You need **dream** no more	A dream is usually associated with something good – this implies that the product will make your dreams come true. Dream: us. assoc. w. s/thing gd. – implies VO5 makes dreams come true
12 **fantastic** wash-in, wash-out colours	
vibrant fashion shades	
your hair will always look its **shiny best**	
costing **just** £5.25	
unique money-back guarantee	
The **ideal** choice	

Activity 5

1 Now that you have studied the advertisement carefully, try rewriting it using *factual* detail only. Start by listing the facts, then link them into sentences to write your own advert.

2 What does your study of the advertisement, and your rewrite of it, show you about:
 • the use of fact and opinion
 • the way language is used to influence the reader?

Practice

Articles written in the sports pages of newspapers often combine fact and opinion. Read the following article closely and then complete Activity 6.

WOULD YOU BELIEVE IT?

Few could have predicted that this fixture would have taken on the enormous importance it has, says IVAN SPECK

OK, hands up. Who put money on Newcastle hanging tough with Arsenal and Manchester United in March?

Of all the joys English football has thrown up in recent years, none has come as unexpectedly or been as welcome as the sight of Bobby Robson and Alan Shearer leading the Toon Army on a merry march through the Premiership. In the monied world that is the modern game, Newcastle are the closest thing to underdogs we are likely to get.

They went top in December with a pulsating victory at Highbury to end their London hoodoo and they'll be champions if they win every game between now and the end of the season. Manchester United, for once, can't do a thing about it. Arsenal can – or, at least, they can put destiny in the hands of United with victory at St James' Park this afternoon.

On the other hand, a home win achieved without long-term injury victim Craig Bellamy could finally ignite Geordie dreams and turn hope into belief on Tyneside.

The two sides meet again a week today, same place, five minutes later and in a different competition, the FA Cup. Would they settle for a win each? Perhaps – but which way round?

Daily Mail

1 From the article, identify and write down:

- three facts
- three opinions
- one opinion stated as a fact
- a sentence in which fact and opinion are mixed together.

2 Look for evidence to suggest that the writer is biased in favour of Newcastle. Copy the chart below and list your evidence, explaining how it shows bias:

Evidence	How it shows bias
'hanging tough'	Suggests Newcastle's a strong team – that could be difficult to beat.
'Of all the joys'	

 POINTS TO REMEMBER

! A *fact* is something that can be proved to be true.

! A *false fact* is something that can be proved to be false.

! An *opinion* is a point of view – it cannot be proved to be true or false.

! *Opinion* can be presented as though it were fact.

! Words can be used to help *disguise opinion*.

! The results of a *survey* can be misleading.

! *Bias* can be created by the way facts are selected and used.

2 Following an argument

One writer may argue in favour of banning violent films on TV. Another may argue that all children should stay at school until the age of seventeen. Yet another may argue that all cigarette advertising should be banned. An *argument* is a series of reasons or points presented to support a particular point of view.

Identifying the key points

The first stage in following an argument is being able to identify the *key points* made by the writer. To do this you need to read closely and summarise the main points. Sometimes you will be able to use the writer's words; sometimes you will need to use your own.

Activity 1

Read the newspaper article that follows. As you read, identify the key points of both arguments, and record them in a chart like the one below. The first few have been done for you.

Simon Hinde: Yes	John Triggs: No
Many professional people smoke cannabis.	Your attitude to cannabis depends on who you listen to.
It is the perfect social drug.	If it had been legal, he would have smoked it in his teens.
Less harmful than alcohol.	Those who smoke cannabis lose their motivation to succeed.

Should cannabis now be legalised?

Home Secretary David Blunkett yesterday announced his intention of re-categorising cannabis so that possession is no longer an arrestable offence. This will be seen by many as the first step on the road to legalisation of the drug – but is it a step that the Government should be taking? Two Express writers give their views.

YES
SIMON HINDE

The other day, the writer John Mortimer disclosed that he had been at a dinner party at which a senior politician, known for his strong moral tone, had produced and smoked a cannabis
5 cigarette. His revelation caused no stir, but then why should it?

MPs smoke cannabis, as do doctors, lawyers (including, I am told on good authority,
10 High Court judges), policemen and teachers. Cannabis is enjoyed for many of the same reasons as alcohol. It is mildly intoxicating, relaxing, a remover of inhibitions, and conducive to good humour and entertaining
15 conversation. It is the perfect social drug. There is some evidence that smoking cannabis damages your health but probably rather less so than alcohol and tobacco. It is certainly less harmful to society than alcohol. After smoking a
20 few joints, users do not roam around the streets in gangs, start fights, or urinate in alleyways.

Nor is cannabis a 'gateway' drug. Users are not psychologically impelled to move on to cocaine, heroin, LSD, ecstasy or any other
25 harder drugs. Certainly some cannabis users do progress to other drugs but this is more likely to be because the illegality of cannabis forces users to get their supply from dealers who have other wares on offer. Legalise cannabis, break
30 the link with the dealer, and you make it less likely, not more, that users will move on to something really damaging.

The other reason why most users of heroin, say, will also have used cannabis is just that
35 cannabis is so widely used. They have probably all had a few drinks in their time, too, but nobody suggests alcohol is a gateway drug, do they?

A huge amount of police time is wasted enforcing the laws on this largely harmless drug.
40 People are taken to court for possession of small amounts of it kept for personal use. Otherwise law-abiding people get a criminal record, courts are clogged up and policemen are diverted from more useful activities. More seriously, sick
45 people who use cannabis to relieve symptoms are persecuted to no purpose.

By keeping cannabis illegal, a booming business is left in the hands of criminals. Some are harmless, even idealistic, dealers, but some
50 are a great deal nastier. Legalise it and most users will instead nip down to the off-licence for a packet of Marlboro Green or Silk Cut High as a Kite, or whatever the tobacco barons call their new product. And, as Gordon Brown
55 cannot fail to have noticed, it will raise billions for the Exchequer. In the area of South London where I live, the police recently announced that, for a trial period, they would not arrest people found in possession of small amounts of
60 cannabis in an experiment that is being watched carefully.

Has the area become more threatening? Of course not. People are a little more open about smoking in pubs and cafés but nothing else
65 seems to have changed. Should cannabis be legalised? Of course it should and David Blunkett has taken a sensible step in the right direction. He is testing public opinion and, all being well, in a year or two will free harmless cannabis
70 smokers altogether from the threat of the law.

NO
JOHN TRIGGS

Cannabis, depending on who you listen to, is either the best plant on the planet or the scourge of our society. When you're growing up your friends tend to give you the first explanation and your parents, your school and the Government give you the second.

Unfortunately, most adolescents believe their friends and ignore their parents and that's exactly what I did.

Until the age of 20, I thought that cannabis was cool though perhaps because it was illegal, I had never come across it. If I had, I would almost certainly have smoked it, acquired a taste for it, and still be smoking it today. As it happens, I didn't really meet it until university. This probably surprises the many people who say that it is everywhere; who say that there is no point in it being illegal because banning it is protecting nobody. By the time I came into contact with it, I had managed to gain the ability to make my own decisions and I decided that I would prefer to stick to lager.

So however prolific the arguments against it, I know for certain that the present law stopped me from smoking cannabis.

Which leaves us only with the question of whether smoking pot is bad for you. We've all heard the arguments against it – cannabis is a gateway to other drugs, it makes you paranoid and can kill off your motivation. 'Rubbish,' say the weedophiles, 'there's no evidence that it leads to other drugs and it doesn't do you any more harm than smoking. Anyway you're all just out to get us.'

In such a minefield of emotionally charged argument, I can again rely only on my own experience. While I didn't smoke it, many of my friends did. In fact, some of them did little else. And while it's true to say that not all of them progressed to hard drugs, a few found that the high they got from cannabis wasn't enough. They started seeking out ecstasy and cocaine; a couple tried heroin.

Without exception, everybody who regularly smoked dope lost their motivation to succeed. I saw students with far superior A-levels to me let first-class degrees slip away because they didn't see the point. Today, few of them use their degrees and many are struggling to find decent jobs. Those who smoked little or no cannabis have, in general, had more success.

However these are generalisations and my university experience would not count as scientific evidence, but when I remember the scientific evidence I have been presented with on issues of public health (BSE, foot and mouth, eggs, that sort of thing) I'm happy to stick to my own anecdotal experience.

My friends smoked it even though it was illegal to do so. Banning it obviously didn't work. This might be true but it's also true that if it wasn't banned I would probably be smoking it and so would many more people like me.

Before we get obsessed with winning an argument with our parents, we should remember that we can't be sure that cannabis isn't dangerous. And if it is, once we legalise it we will never be able to turn back the clock.

Recognising techniques

Writers develop their arguments in different ways. To follow how the argument is constructed, you need to recognise some of the more commonly used techniques:

Techniques used for argument	Examples of techniques
Rhetorical questions These are questions to which no answer is required. They are often used for dramatic effect and to draw the reader in.	'His revelation caused no stir, but then why should it?' [Simon Hinde lines 6–7]
Anecdotal evidence This is personal evidence, usually in the form of a short account of an incident (an anecdote), that is used to support a point.	'While I didn't smoke it, many of my friends did. In fact, some of them did little else. And while it's true to say that not all of them progressed to hard drugs, a few found that the high they got from cannabis wasn't enough.' [John Triggs lines 109–13]
Facts Writers may refer to facts to support the points they make.	'People are taken to court for possession of small amounts of it [cannabis] kept for personal use.' [Simon Hinde lines 40–41]
Opinions It's important to recognise that an argument is almost always based on opinion and the writer's interpretation of the 'facts'. Remember: opinion will often be stated as though it is fact.	'Certainly, some cannabis users do progress to other drugs but this is more likely to be because the illegality of cannabis forces users to get their supply from dealers who have other wares on offer.' [Simon Hinde lines 25–9] 'A huge amount of police time is wasted enforcing the laws on this largely harmless drug.' [Simon Hinde lines 38–9]
Generalisations Personal experience or facts are used to form general conclusions.	'Those who smoked little or no cannabis have, in general, had more success.' [John Triggs lines 121–22]
Counter argument Writers may present a view which is an alternative to their own and then say something to 'counter' or go against it.	'This probably surprises the many people who say that it is everywhere.' [John Triggs lines 87–8]

Now re-read the article. Look for and note down *at least two* more examples of *each* of the techniques listed in the chart opposite:

- rhetorical questions
- anecdotal evidence
- facts
- opinions
- generalisations
- counter argument.

Evaluating an argument

Once you have identified the key points of an argument, and understood how the argument has been constructed, you are ready to *evaluate* it. To do this you need to ask some questions and to challenge the assumptions that are made. Here are some of the things you might question or challenge in Simon Hinde's argument:

What the writer says	Questions you might ask
'It is certainly less harmful to society than alcohol.' (lines 18–19)	Is that a valid reason for legalising it – just because it's **less** harmful?
'A huge amount of police time is wasted enforcing the laws on this largely harmless drug.' (lines 38–9)	Is dealing with traffic offences a better use of police time?
'By keeping cannabis illegal, a booming business is left in the hands the criminals.' (lines 47–8)	So? Why not deal with the criminals? We don't shut shops because there are shoplifters.
'Legalise it and most users will instead nip down to the off-licence for a packet of Marlboro Green or Silk Cut High as a Kite, or whatever the tobacco barons call their new product.' (lines 50–54)	Is it a good thing that the tobacco barons could make even more money than they already do?
'People are a little more open about smoking in pubs and cafés ...' (lines 63–4)	What about the impression that this gives to children who learn by example?

Activity **3**

Re-read the argument by John Triggs. Make a copy of the chart above and fill it in with **five** questions you could ask about points he makes.

Asking questions like this will help you to develop your own point of view. As a reader, it is important that you should question what you read and form your own opinions on it.

Practice

1 Read the following editorial, which was written in response to the evidence that girls were achieving more at school than boys. As you read it for the first time, identify and list:

- the key points
- facts and opinions.

2 Re-read the article and discuss, with a partner or in a group, the questions that surround the text. Make notes for your answers to them.

The school system that gives girls an advantage

Examination evidence shows that girls are outpacing boys. What are we to make of this? The easy answer is to accept the

5 feminist claim that girls would always equal or surpass boys when the education system was rid of its 'male bias'. But things are not that simple. Nor that

10 trivial.

As it happens, the results do reflect the impact of woolly educational thinking, which has played down actual

15 examinations and elevated classroom performance through coursework. This gives girls an advantage, since their greater keenness and biddability tend to

20 earn them higher marks than more naturally rebellious and individualistic boys.

It is not a question of begrudging girls their success. To

25 do so would be unfair and stupid. But society is best served when the great majority of boys are able to emerge from eleven years of compulsory schooling with the

30 emotional and intellectual equipment to find meaningful jobs and roles.

Other factors – family breakdown, absent fathers, the corrupting effects of welfare 35 dependency – are already helping to create a pool of anti-social and jobless young men who prey on society. These are the burglars, muggers and car thieves whose 40 activities do so much to drag down our quality of life. The 'feminisation' of the school system, with its prizes-for-all ethos, will simply push more 45 young men into this pool.

So, yes, let us hear it for the girls. They have done what was demanded of them – and well. But if there is not a return to tests 50 which challenge a pupil to show what he or she has in his head, we shall surely be hearing *from* the boys. And we shall not like what we hear. 55

Side questions:

What technique is being used here?

What is being implied by the use of the word 'trivial'?

Is this fact or opinion?

Does the writer begrudge girls their success? Is he 'unfair and stupid'?

Are girls affected by these things?

What technique being used here?

Is this consistent? Hasn't the writer already suggested that there are no 'prizes' for boys?

What does this imply about the current tests and about girls?

What does the writer imply in the final sentence?

Daily Express

Identifying bias in an argument

Bias is shown in people's opinions when personal feelings are allowed to influence their judgement. It can be evident in the words writers use to put across a particular point of view:

Activity 5

1 Re-read this extract from **The school system that gives girls the advantage**. Match the annotations listed below to the appropriate words and phrases in the extract.

> As it happens, the results do reflect the impact of woolly educational thinking, which has played down actual examinations and elevated classroom performance through coursework. This gives girls an advantage, since their greater keenness and biddability tend to earn them higher marks than more naturally rebellious and individualistic boys.

a a phrase which implies examinations have been made to seem less important

b a word which suggests classroom performance is overrated

c a phrase which implies an over-willingness to please and obey

d a word which suggests the thinking is unclear and lacks substance

e a phrase which suggests a sense of strength, toughness and adventure

2 Complete this sentence correctly:

   By using language in this way the writer reinforces his opinion that:
   - Girls work harder than boys.
   - Classroom performance and coursework are more important than exams.
   - Schools are failing boys and they deserve better.

3 Find at least four more examples of evidence of bias in the article on page 22. Copy each sentence in which the examples occur and annotate them to show what is being implied or suggested.

Activity 6

How does the writer present his argument in *The school system that gives girls an advantage?*

To answer this, you need to write five paragraphs in which you:
1 Describe the key points.
2 Comment on the use of fact and/or opinion.
3 Comment on the techniques used.
4 Show how bias is evident.
5 Evaluate the argument by challenging some of the points made.

POINTS TO REMEMBER !

! An *argument* is usually based on a mixture of fact and opinion.

! To follow an argument you need to identify the *key points*.

! Writers use a *range of techniques* to help them develop their arguments.

! *Bias* can be evident in an argument in the selection of detail and the way the writer uses words to imply things.

! To *evaluate an argument* you need to ask questions about it and challenge the assumptions that are made by the writer.

Purpose and audience

The first two things writers need to consider when they start to write are:

Purpose
Why am I writing this?
What do I want to achieve?
How am I going to achieve this?

Audience
Who am I writing this for?
Is anyone else likely to read it?
How can I get my readers' attention?

When you are reading a text you need to:
- identify the intended purpose(s) and audience(s)
- assess how successful the writer has been in targeting these.

Read the following advertisement carefully.

1 Here are the questions the writer needed to ask about *purpose* and *audience*. Try to work out what the answers were and complete the chart below.

Questions	Answers
Why am I writing this?	
What do I want to achieve?	
How am I going to achieve this?	
Who am I writing this for?	
Is anyone else likely to read it?	
How can I get their attention?	

2 Complete these sentences:
   a The intended purpose of the writer of the advertisement is ...
   b The intended audience of the writer of the advertisement is ...

3 Do you think the writer has been successful in targeting purpose and audience? Give *four* reasons for your answer.

WARNING:

CLEAR SKIN CAN SERIOUSLY IMPROVE YOUR CHANCES

So you won't want your chances ruined because of spots. What causes them? Well, pesky spot-causing bacteria breed in clogged pores, but OXY Pads help unclog your pores and open them up to the air. And because the little critters hate oxygen, those bacteria can't survive. So don't worry about getting spots before the big party, let OXY Pads help prevent them, leaving you to knock 'em dead.

DON'T RUIN YOUR CHANCES

OXY is a registered trade mark of the GlaxoSmithKline Group of Companies.

OXY
36 DUO PADS

Presentation

Appearance is often an important factor in the success of a text. There is a range of *presentational devices* that writers and designers can use to give a text more visual impact:

- **Illustrations, including photographs and drawings**, are often used to add interest, information and variety to a text.

- **Colours** are used because they can directly affect the way the reader responds to a text. Certain colours tend to be linked with particular moods, ideas and objects. Take the colour red:

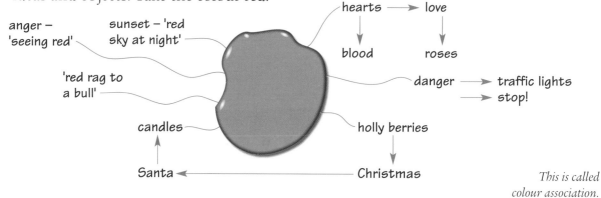

This is called colour association.

- **Captions** can sometimes be used to give a brief explanation of, or comment on, a picture. This may guide the reader to look more closely at it. Discuss the connection between the photograph and the caption below:

Roy Keane leapfrogs above his United colleague David Beckham in the pay stakes, but Beckham could soon overtake him.
The Times

Often it is the caption which gives the picture its meaning. Write two other captions that could be used to give this picture very different meanings.

This technique of fixing the meaning of a picture by the words you place with it is known as *anchoring*.

Activity 2

Look again at the advertisement on the previous page.

1. How do the illustrations:
   - link to the writing
   - provide information in a visual form
   - add interest to the text?

2. Why do you think the designer chose these colours? What impact do they have?

- **Charts and diagrams** enable the writer to present complex information in a simplified form.

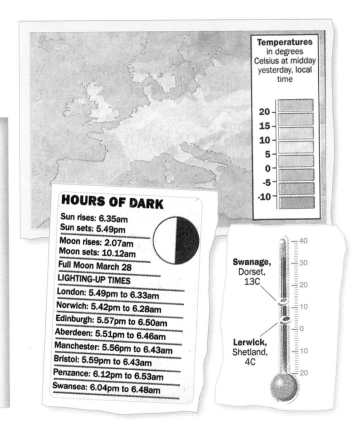

HOURS OF DARK

Sun rises: 6.35am
Sun sets: 5.49pm

Moon rises: 2.07am
Moon sets: 10.12am

Full Moon March 28

LIGHTING-UP TIMES

London: 5.49pm to 6.33am
Norwich: 5.42pm to 6.28am
Edinburgh: 5.57pm to 6.50am
Aberdeen: 5.51pm to 6.46am
Manchester: 5.56pm to 6.43am
Bristol: 5.59pm to 6.43am
Penzance: 6.12pm to 6.53am
Swansea: 6.04pm to 6.48am

Temperatures in degrees Celsius at midday yesterday, local time

20
15
10
5
0
-5
-10

Swanage, Dorset, 13C

Lerwick, Shetland, 4C

Activity 3

1 Look at the *charts* and *diagrams* about the weather. For each one, think about:
   - the information you are given
   - the use of facts and figures
   - how this information would be presented using only words
   - the ways in which they help the reader make comparisons.

2 Make a list of five points which explain why and when writers might use charts and diagrams.

- **Logos and slogans**

  Many companies and charities have their own emblem or trademark by which they can be easily identified. This is known as the *logo*. They may also use a distinctive phrase, again as a mark of identity. This is known as the *slogan*.

Activity 4

Make a collection of well-known *logos* and *slogans*, noting down the association and explaining what is suggested by each one.

Logo or slogan	Associated with	What it suggests
⭕⭕⭕	Olympic games	Unity – working together – shared interests
Because you're worth it	L'Oreal	

- **A range of *fonts*, <u>styles</u>, SIZES and effects**

  These are used to:
  - distinguish one word or phrase from another
  - emphasise a particular word or point.

Activity 5

1 Identify and list the different types of font style and other visual effects used in the following text.
2 Describe how the writer has used these to:
   - distinguish between points
   - emphasise a particular point.

drugs & sport

SPORT ENGLAND

Football Association

Whether you're into football, athletics, swimming or basketball, you'll know it takes practice and hard work to reach a good standard. If you want to succeed in sport, fitness and concentration are as important as talent.

Drugs and sport don't mix

Sports people who mess with drugs are destroying their chances of success. They tend to get more injuries, lose energy and start missing sessions. Fitness and concentration go downhill fast. Not only has drug use ruined promising careers, the image of sport suffers.

What about steroids?

You've probably heard of people who have taken drugs like anabolic steroids to make them perform better or to change their body image. Not only do they risk being banned from the sport, they are messing with their health. Anabolic steroids can stop your body developing properly and cause serious health problems. Sport is about fair competition. Not only is taking anabolic steroids dangerous – it is CHEATING.

Enjoy sport – be drug free!

Name: anabolic steroids

PRODUCT NAMES
Deca-Durabolin, Dianabol, Stanozolol
WHAT THEY LOOK LIKE
tablets or oily liquids
HOW THEY'RE TAKEN
Tablets are swallowed; liquids are injected into muscle.
WHY SOME PEOPLE TAKE THIS DRUG
If taken over a long period of time and combined with exercise, anabolic steroids may make people more muscular.
WHAT THE RISKS ARE
Taking anabolic steroids can really damage health and stop young people growing properly. They can make boys grow breasts and make girls grow more body hair.

14

15

- **Headlines**

Writers aim to capture the reader's interest with their headlines. To do this they often use a range of techniques.

I thought we would never get out alive

Daily Mail

Who will trust the spin doctors now?

Sunday Post

Dyeing for a Boy-band-binge Weekend

Shaders & Toners, Wella

United's double act shatters sorry Spurs

Daily Express

Activity 6

1 Look closely at the headlines. Which one:

- uses a rhetorical question
- is made to sound dramatic
- uses alliteration
- uses a play on words (a pun)?

Copy and complete the following chart by identifying the technique(s) used and saying what the effect is. The first one is done for you:

Headline	Technique(s)	Effect
'I thought we would never get out alive'	Made to sound dramatic	Emphasises the danger and the seriousness of the incident
'Who will trust the spin doctors now?'		

2 Make a collection of headlines from newspaper and magazine articles, leaflets and advertisements. Aim to collect headlines that are striking and interesting. Identify the technique(s) used in each headline.

- **Sub-headings** are used to:
  - separate the text into smaller more easily managed units
  - summarise key points
  - emphasise a particular point.

- **Bullet points** are used to list points in a condensed form.

Activity 7

1 Read the following extract. The numbers 1, 2 and 3 have been substituted for the sub-headings in the original text. Match the most appropriate sub-heading from the following list to the number. For each one, give a reason for your choice.

a Take up jogging	**d** Lose weight fast
b Don't watch the clock	**e** Keep active
c Keep the weight off	**f** Plan your diet

2 Rewrite paragraph 2 using bullet points. You will need to think carefully about wording.

HOW TO LOSE WEIGHT

Follow our tips to a long-term solution – it can be done

By following any diet – no matter how weird or wonderful – most people will lose weight in the short-term. The difficult part is to keep the weight off and not get
5 *caught in a cycle of on–off dieting*

1

First, set yourself a target weight. If you've got a lot of weight to lose, set interim targets, to keep your spirits up. Be realistic about how quickly you lose weight. You're likely to
10 lose weight faster at the outset, but a weight loss of just 1lb to 2lb a week is recommended as the maximum for most people. Rapid weight loss is bad for you.

2

Eat foods that are rich in nutrients – so plenty of fruit and vegetables, and starch 15 foods like pasta and potatoes. Cut down on foods that are high in energy with few nutrients, such as fried snack foods. But don't try to cut out your favourite foods altogether. Strict rules can trigger failure. 20

3

It's also important to be active. But that doesn't mean you have to join a gym or take up jogging – any type of exercise is beneficial. Just walk instead of getting the bus or use the stairs instead of the escalator. 25

Structure

Sometimes a writer needs to consider how to position the text on the page to make maximum impact, and how to use presentational devices to achieve this.

Activity 8

1 Look back at **Drugs & sport** on page 28, and make notes on:
   - what each section tells you
   - how the heading and sub-headings are used to organise ideas
   - what the photographs show
   - their positions in the text.

2 Using your notes, write a paragraph:
   - describing how the text is organised
   - commenting on its effectiveness.

Structure is also about the order in which the detail is presented to the reader. To assess this you need to think about why a writer starts in a particular place and the way the ideas are sequenced and linked after that.

Newspaper reports usually answer at least five different questions. These are sometimes called the *five Ws*:

- **W**ho is the story about?
- **W**hat is the story about?
- **W**here did the story take place?
- **W**hen did the story happen?
- **W**hy is the story news?

Journalists are trained to write articles and news stories in a particular way. This is sometimes known as the *news triangle approach*:

1 **The main idea and the vital information**
2 *The details, still important but not essential*
3 The extra information helpful to the story but which might need to be cut

Read the following news report closely.

1 Find and note:
- the answers to the *five Ws*
- **where** the answers appear in the text.

2 Divide the story into the three stages of the *triangle approach*. Where does each stage start and stop?

Jilted lover wrapped up like a 'mummy'

A jilted lover ended up being wrapped like a 'mummy' when tourists stepped in to prevent him causing further mayhem in
5 Masham Market Place.

Christopher Palfrey had just driven 150 miles to the market town when tourists, including an Australian couple, saw him
10 hanging on the door of a car with a young woman desperately trying to escape his clutches.

Eyewitnesses said 33-year-old Palfrey crashed his van into a wall
15 and was then seen hanging on to the outside passenger door of his former girlfriend's car as she drove round the Market Square before smashing into another vehicle.
20 As she tried to run away from him, community-spirited shop staff, businessmen and visitors alerted the police to the mayhem before stepping in to take action.
25 'It happened outside my pub,' said landlady Mandy Ward of the Bay Horse. 'There was a terrific thud and apparently all hell was let loose. An Australian couple
30 then helped to arrest the man trying to get into the woman's car. Fortunately there were road works nearby and it appears everyone rallied round,' she said.

35 'I understand they dragged the man to the ground and tied him up using the red and white plastic tape surrounding the road works to bind him like a mummy.'
40 Palfrey was eventually dumped in the road and, while one person sat on him, others directed the traffic round him until the police arrived.
45 On Wednesday, Palfrey, of The Avenue, Acocks Green, Birmingham, pleaded guilty at Northallerton Magistrates' Court to charges arising from the
50 incident last August, including using threatening behaviour.

He also admitted being a disqualified driver and driving with excess alcohol and without
55 insurance.

Charges of assaulting Australian holidaymakers Joanne and Ian Sherwin were not proceeded with after prosecutor Jane Cook said
60 they had now returned home. Palfrey, who also pleaded guilty to further offences committed in Birmingham, was remanded on bail for the preparation of
65 probation and medical reports. Magistrates ordered that he must not visit North Yorkshire until his next court appearance.

Northallerton, Thirsk and Bedale Times

In the report, paragraphs are used to help organise the material. They are closely linked by content. Re-read the opening two paragraphs. The highlights show you the links:

1 Copy these paragraphs and also the third and fourth paragraphs. Highlight the links between them.

2 Christopher Palfrey is referred to five times in the first two paragraphs:

A jilted lover/him/Christopher Palfrey/ him/his

List all the other references in the article. Why do you think he is referred to differently at different times?

> A jilted lover ended up being wrapped like a 'mummy' when tourists stepped in to prevent him
> 5 causing further mayhem in Masham Market Place.
>   Christopher Palfrey had just driven 150 miles to the market town when
> 10 tourists, including an Australian couple, saw him hanging on the door of a car with a young woman desperately trying
> 15 to escape his clutches.

Language

Many writers choose to write in standard English, which is the form taught in schools. Within that form, or as an alternative to it, they may use a range of linguistic devices which you need to be able to recognise and discuss.

Read the following chart carefully.

1 Look at the examples in the third column. Explain how each example shows how the linguistic device works.

2 Look through a range of magazines and newspapers. Find *at least two* more examples of each of the linguistic devices listed in the chart.

Linguistic devices	When and why a writer would use it	An example
Colloquialisms: words or phrases appropriate to conversation and other informal occasions – a feature of non-standard English.	Often used in magazines and plays a large part in on-line messaging and texting. Aims to address the reader directly and make them involved.	'You're feeling a bit frustrated at the mo', 'cause there's lots of stuff you wanna get done and you don't seem to be making much progress.'

Linguistic devices	When and why a writer would use it	An example
Tabloidese: tends to have by restricted vocabulary range, highly compressed language and heavy use of puns and wordplay.	A feature of writing in the tabloid press. Used to present information in a shortened form and to entertain the reader.	**'Grandad raps yob girl mum.'**
Rhetoric: characterised by rhetorical questions, repetition, lists of three and exaggeration.	Appears mainly in speeches and in texts written to persuade or argue.	'What is happening to Britain? One man is stabbed for wearing a Rolex. One girl is shot for texting on her mobile. One gran is battered for the pennies in her purse. And no one seems to care.'
Loaded language: words are used to present a particular point of view.	Frequently found in newspaper reports. They reveal bias on the part of the writer and the intention to persuade the reader to a particular point of view.	'The soldiers were among six heroes killed as they tried to shoot their way to safety after their Chinook was blasted out of the sky.'
Technical language: words and phrases specific to subject matter that may not be familiar to the reader.	Often found in advertisements where the writer wishes to impress the reader with technical information about the product.	'A highly effective dermatological shampoo containing salicylic acid (to remove stubborn flakes) and piroctone olamine (to soothe itching). Can be used up to four times a week.'
Emotive language: words are chosen to arouse emotion in the reader.	Widely used in a range of non-fiction texts such as magazines, newspapers, charity advertisements and autobiographies.	'It's an *outrage* to leave vulnerable kids like these out on the streets, a prey to the cruelty of the winter weather and to every unsavoury character who offers them "help".'

Practice: Writing about media text

In an examination you will be asked to write about the *media features* of a text. The main areas you will need to focus on are:

- purpose and audience
- presentation and layout
- structure and meaning
- linguistic devices.

Look back to remind yourself of the main points of this unit before working through Activity 11 to help you to assess the media features of the text opposite.

Activity 12

Read the newspaper article that follows and answer these questions:

1. Identify the *purpose(s)* of this article. Give evidence to support each point you make.

2. What different things can you work out about the *intended audience* of this article?

3. How are the *illustrations* used to reinforce the message of the article?

4. Explain how the *sub-headings* are used to:
   - separate the text
   - emphasise a particular point.

5. How does the writer use a *range of fonts and effects* to reinforce his message?

6. How does the writer use the following *linguistic devices* to help achieve his purpose:
   - emotive language
   - rhetoric
   - loaded language?

7. Re-read your answers to questions 1–5. How effective do you think this article is in:
   - its presentation
   - how the choice of language is likely to influence the reader's response?

   Give clear reasons for your answers.

POINTS TO REMEMBER

When writing about a text you need to identify and discuss:

! the intended purpose(s) and audience(s) and the writer's success in targeting them

! the range of presentational devices that writers and designers have used

! the way the text is positioned on the page

! the order in which the detail is presented to the reader

! the range of linguistic devices used by the writer.

'GREAT AND GOOD' HAVE BLOOD ON THEIR HANDS

We're used to hearing pompous, puerile drivel from the mouths of lawyers.

But David Bean QC, chairman of the Bar Council and leader of 10,000 barristers, has gone too far. 5

He warns that Britain could go down 'the slippery slope' and become a police state if the scales of justice were 'unbalanced'. 10

Wake up, Mr Bean.

The scales of justice are already unbalanced – **TIPPED IN THE FAVOUR OF THE WRONGDOERS**. 15

We've already gone down a slippery slope – **INTO AN ABYSS OF MURDER AND MAYHEM**.

Typical

Once the streets of Britain were ruled by the power of the PC – the Police Constable. 20

In Britain today, violent drug addicts are walking the streets looking for their next victim. Because some smart-arsed lawyer has sprung them from court on a fine point of law or used silky words to persuade a court to go soft. 25

DO THEY REALLY CARE THAT PEOPLE THE LENGTH AND BREADTH OF BRITAIN ARE SCARED?

We see society crumbling before our eyes with the police, for all their hard and brave work, 30 powerless to stop the rot.

Horrific

It hasn't always been this bad. Once there was a hope…

Nine years ago, a young, almost unknown 35 politician stood before his party conference and declared:

'Labour is the party of law and order. Tough on crime and tough on the causes of crime.'

Today Tony Blair is in Downing Street, but 40 Britain is a dangerous crime zone.

His well-meant promise has been nicked from under his nose.

Horrific crimes with a callous 45 indifference to life dominate the news day after scary day.

A GIRL is shot in the head by a youth who steals her mobile phone.

A MAN is stabbed to death by a 50 thief who wants his Rolex watch.

CHILDREN are kidnapped by a gang who steal their mother's expensive car.

Shootings are so commonplace 55 in big cities that they're not big news any more – and scarcely rate a mention in the Press or on the TV news.

SO WHAT'S THE ANSWER? 60

Many people talk about 'doing a New York' and copying Sir Rudy Giuliani's brilliantly successful crime war.

Sadly, they fail to recognise the huge difference between New York and London politics. 65

Over there, Rudy was able to **BUILD MORE PRISONS**.

What he did was simple: **HE** locked up the bad guys. Rudy also had the power to order his police chief to clear up crime no matter what. 70

He poured thousands more cops on to the streets with zero tolerance of **ALL** offences.

Tough

In Britain, no one knows where the buck stops – except everyone says: 'Not with me.' 75

We **CAN** beat crime. But only if we have the guts to finance a police force that can do the job. We need politicians, both local and national, to run for office on tough crime agendas **AND MEAN IT**. 80

If they do, they will do what Rudy did – and win again and again.

Sun

Generally we can identify different types of texts very quickly. For example, we can usually recognise an advertisement just by looking at it. We don't need to read it to know *what* it is. The same is true of many other types of texts. We make judgements about them very quickly, based on their appearance.

Activity 1

Look at, but do not read, the following four texts. Complete the chart below for each text:

Text	Type of text	Where you might find it	Evidence for decisions
A	Dictionary definition	Dictionary – probably for adults	Layout – bold print – italic – list – numbered explanations
B			
C			
D			

Once you have completed your chart compare it with a partner's. Were some more difficult than others? If so, why?

A

fash+ion ('fæʃən) n. **1. a.** style in clothes, cosmetics, behaviour, etc., esp. the latest or most admired style. **b.** (*as modifier*): *fashion magazine*. **2. a.** manner of performance; mode; way: *a striking fashion*. **b.** (*in combination*): *crab-fashion*. **3.** a way of life that revolves around the activities, 5 dress, interests, etc. that are most fashionable. **4.** shape, appearance, or form. **5.** sort; kind; type. **6. after** *or* **in a fashion. a.** in some manner, but not very well: *I mended it, after a fashion*. **b.** of a low order, of a sort: *he is a poet, after a fashion*. **7. after the fashion of.** like, similar to. **8. of fashion.** of high social standing. ~*vb.* (*tr.*) to give a particular form to. **10.** to make 10 suitable or fitting. **11.** *Obsolete.* to contrive; manage. [C13 *facioun* form, manner from Old French *faceon*, from Latin *facti ō* a making, from *facere* to make] — '**fash+ion+er** *n.*

B

SPORTSWEAR

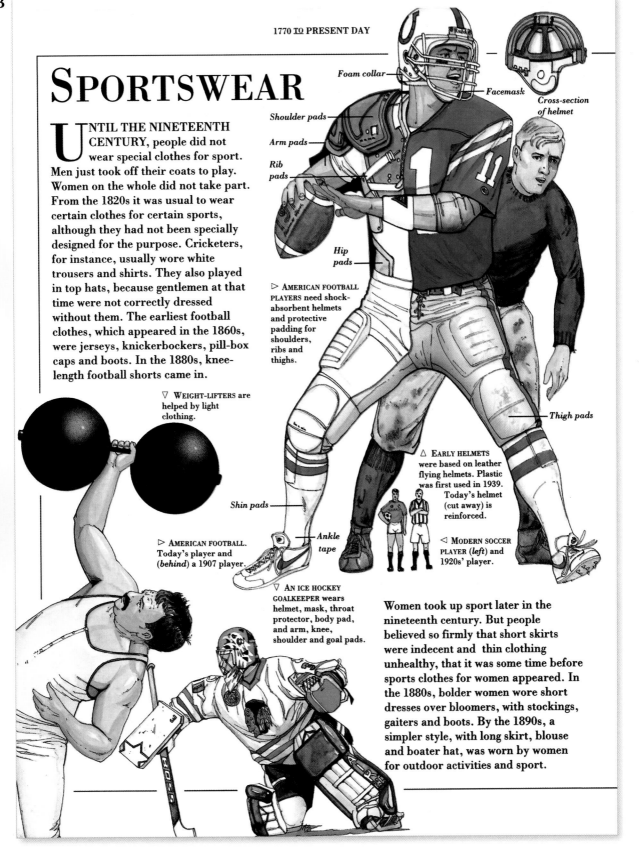

UNTIL THE NINETEENTH CENTURY, people did not wear special clothes for sport. Men just took off their coats to play. Women on the whole did not take part. From the 1820s it was usual to wear certain clothes for certain sports, although they had not been specially designed for the purpose. Cricketers, for instance, usually wore white trousers and shirts. They also played in top hats, because gentlemen at that time were not correctly dressed without them. The earliest football clothes, which appeared in the 1860s, were jerseys, knickerbockers, pill-box caps and boots. In the 1880s, knee-length football shorts came in.

Foam collar

Facemask

Cross-section of helmet

Shoulder pads

Arm pads

Rib pads

Hip pads

△ AMERICAN FOOTBALL PLAYERS need shock-absorbent helmets and protective padding for shoulders, ribs and thighs.

▽ WEIGHT-LIFTERS are helped by light clothing.

Thigh pads

△ EARLY HELMETS were based on leather flying helmets. Plastic was first used in 1939. Today's helmet (cut away) is reinforced.

Shin pads

▷ AMERICAN FOOTBALL. Today's player and (behind) a 1907 player.

Ankle tape

◁ MODERN SOCCER PLAYER (left) and 1920s' player.

▽ AN ICE HOCKEY GOALKEEPER wears helmet, mask, throat protector, body pad, and arm, knee, shoulder and goal pads.

Women took up sport later in the nineteenth century. But people believed so firmly that short skirts were indecent and thin clothing unhealthy, that it was some time before sports clothes for women appeared. In the 1880s, bolder women wore short dresses over bloomers, with stockings, gaiters and boots. By the 1890s, a simpler style, with long skirt, blouse and boater hat, was worn by women for outdoor activities and sport.

dilemmas Virginia Ironside

THIS WEEK'S PROBLEM:
Marina has a problem with her children's appearances. Her 14-year-old son is planning to get a ring through his nose, with or without his parent's permission; her 12-year-old daughter wears mini-skirts so short her bottom shows. Marina wants to give them their freedom but she doesn't know how far she should go

Adolescent children are fantastically self-conscious about their appearance. They'll wear nothing that isn't dead right for their crowd. That's why, if you buy them a green jersey of the wrong green, or a pair of socks covered with musical notes that you think are 'fun' and they think are naff, they often simply refuse to wear them.

So when Marina's children decide to take certain design decisions, she can be certain that in their own circle they'll look absolutely spot on. She may think they look weird; their friends will think they look the bee's knees.

The fact that *she* thinks they look provocative or brutal is beside the point. Who cares what adults think? A gang of skinheads is hardly likely to pounce on a boy just because of a ring in his nose; they'll have far more sympathy with Marina's young son that Marina herself. Little girls who show their bums in the street may get wolf-whistles and leery looks, but rapists' victims, if newspaper pictures are anything to go by, are more likely to be wearing trackie bottoms or school uniforms than revealing little numbers.

In the sixties, I was one of the first to wear mini-skirts, long black boots and fish-net stockings. The look shrieked 'tart' in a far louder voice then than any mini-skirt from Jigsaw would today. Nothing ever happened to me because of my clothes.

Marina must remember not only her own teenage whims but also how irritating it was when her children begged her not to wear certain things to pick them up from school. 'Oh, Mum, you look so weird in those funny trousers ...' was the wail from my son when I went a bit mad on some ghastly, never-to-be-worn-again breeches.

But as we, as parents, tone down our dress when in the company of our children and their friends to save them dreadful embarrassment, it's quite right that our children should do the same when around our contemporaries – or their grandparents. Longer skirts. Nose-ring temporarily removed. But, generally, dress is a harmless way of expressing individuality. If Marina forces her kids into V-necked jumpers and clean jeans, their individuality will only express itself in other, far more dangerous ways. Neat as pins on the outside; probably stoned to the eyebrows on the inside.

Marina can express her anxieties, but after that she should shut up as she starts to practise the difficult new 'hands-off' parenting of the adolescent. 'It's only a phase,' she can remind herself. Only too soon, sadly, her children are going to look pretty much exactly the same as all the other young men and women in the street.

from *Essential Articles 4*, The Resource File for Issues, Carel Press

Miss S.'s daily emergence from the van was highly dramatic. Suddenly and without warning the rear door would be flung open to reveal the tattered draperies that masked the terrible interior. There was a pause, then through the veils would be hurled several bulging plastic sacks.
5 Another pause, before slowly and with great caution one sturdy slippered leg came feeling for the floor before the other followed and one had the first sight of the day's wardrobe. Hats were always a feature: a black railwayman's hat with a long neb worn slightly on the skew so that she looked like a drunken signalman or a French guardsman of the
10 1880s; there was her Charlie Brown pitcher's hat; and in June 1977 an octagonal straw table-mat, tied on with a chiffon scarf and a bit of cardboard for the peak. She also went in for green eyeshades. Her skirts had a telescopic appearance, as they had often been lengthened many times over by the simple expedient of sewing a strip of extra cloth around the
15 hem, though with no attempt at matching. One skirt was made by sewing several orange dusters together. When she fell foul of authority she put it down to her clothes. Once, late at night, the police rang me from Tunbridge Wells. They had picked her up on the station, thinking her dress was a nightie. She was indignant. 'Does it look like a nightie?
20 You see lots of people wearing dresses like this. I don't think this style can have got to Tunbridge Wells yet.'

Writing Home by Alan Bennett

Skimming a text

Sometimes we need to read the whole of a text quickly in order to get a general idea of what it is about. This type of quick reading is called *skimming*. When we skim a text we are focusing on the surface detail only.

Activity 2

Skim **Texts A–D** to discover:

• what they are about   • the intended purpose and audience.

Your aim is to read the texts as quickly as possible. Enter your findings on a chart like this:

Text	What it is about	Intended purpose and audience
A	Various alternative meanings of the word 'fashion'	People who want to discover the word's meanings and/or spelling
B		

The ability to skim a text is an important skill which improves with practice.

Scanning a text

Sometimes you need to find a particular detail in a text. To do this you would not read the whole text closely – you would scan it. When you scan a text, your eyes move quickly over its surface until they focus on a significant word or phrase. Then you stop and read more closely to check it is the detail you require. *Scanning* is the skill you use when you read timetables or the evening's TV guide.

Activity 3

Scan **Texts A–D** to find the answers to the following questions. Make brief notes for your answers and keep a record of how long it takes you.

1 What were the earliest football clothes?

2 What kind of hat did Miss S. wear in June 1977?

3 When was plastic first used in American Football helmets?

4 What was made by sewing several orange dusters together?

5 What problem does Marina have with her children?

6 Why did it take some time for sports clothes for women to appear?

7 Whose son complained that she looked weird 'in those funny trousers'.

8 What is meant by the phrase 'after the fashion of'?

Collating material

Sometimes you will be asked questions that require you to refer to more than one text.

To do this you will need to select and use information from different texts. You will need to:

- use your skills in skimming and scanning
- take useful notes.

Making notes

We all develop our own way of taking notes. Our method changes and improves with practice. The important things to remember about taking notes are that they should be:

- brief
- suited to the purpose for which they are needed.

Look at **Text B** on sportswear again. If you are making notes for your teacher to show your understanding of the text, they might be written like this:

> Text B – probably encyclopaedia or reference – uses illustration
> special clothes for sport introduced in 19th century
> men's clothes for cricket and football were first – details given
> some changes for women in the 1880s and 90s
> details of contemporary American Football outfit
> 1907 player shown in contrast
> weight-lifter and ice hockey goalkeeper also shown

For your own use, you could shorten these further by using abbreviations and hyphens and missing out more words, for example:

> B – prob. ency. or ref. – illus.
> C19 – sport clothes intro.

Alternatively your notes might look like this:

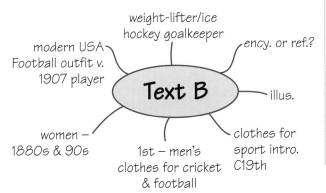

Activity 4

Make your own notes on what **Text C** shows you about teenagers' attitudes to clothes. Make them brief and useful.

Activity 5

Use details from **Texts A**, **B**, **C** and **D** to help you write an answer to this question:

What do you learn from these texts about fashion?

Here are some prompts to help you:

- Definition of fashion: Text A
- How fashions change: Texts B, C
- Clothes as an expression of individuality: Texts C, D
- Different attitudes to fashion: Texts B, C, D

Add your own ideas to these prompts before starting to write. Aim to write about 300 words in your answer.

Comparing texts

Sometimes you may be asked to *compare texts*. To do this you need to examine the similarities and differences between them. The following passage compares **Text B** and **Text C** with regard to:

- purpose and audience
- presentation
- content.

The passage is organised into three short paragraphs, each dealing separately with one bullet point. The annotations show you how the comparison is constructed. Read the paragraphs carefully.

written in the present tense

Establishes purpose and audience of Text B

'However' is used to emphasise a difference between the texts

Another difference is highlighted in the final sentence

Opening sentence shows that emphasis will be on similarities

Examples from both texts are used to support the comparison

Opening statements linking the texts

Establishes purpose and audience of Text C

Uses 'therefore' to sum up differences

The word 'both' is repeated at the start of the second sentence to emphasise a similarity between the texts

'Similarly' is used to emphasise a likeness between the texts

'also' is used to indicate another point of similarity

On the surface these two texts seem to be very different. Text B is clearly written for a reference book of some kind and is probably aimed at a secondary school audience. Its purpose is to inform the reader about sportswear. Text C, on the other hand, seems to be some kind of problem page that would appear in a newspaper. The writer's purpose is to advise Marina, and other parents, on how to deal with teenagers' apearances. The texts are therefore different in form and intended purpose and audience.

Both texts have a number of presentational features. They both carry a heading in large bold print and the writing is presented in columns. Text C carries a photograph of the writer and a sub-heading which outlines the problem to which she is replying. Text B, however, relies more heavily on illustration with a range of annotated drawings of men in sportswear. These illustrations relate directly to the content of the writing whereas the photograph in Text B does not.

Whilst they seem quite different there are similarities between them. They both show that clothes and appearance are important in the impression they create. In the 1820s, for example, cricketers wore top hats because they were not considered 'properly dressed' without them. Similarly, Virginia Ironside makes the point that both adults and children should 'tone down' their clothes when in different company to save 'dreadful embarrassment'. Both texts also make the point that clothes are not just about practicality but about acceptability. Women in the 1890s wore long skirts, blouses and boater hats for sports so as not to be considered indecent. According to Virginia Ironside, modern teenagers will wear only what is 'dead right for their crowd'.

Practice

Skim this article to get a general idea of what it's about and then work through Activity 6.

Sliding Dior Galliano mixes his styles

Jess Carter-Morley
Fashion editor in Paris

John Galliano's haute-couture show for Christian Dior yesterday was as close to a circus as it is possible to get without installing a trapeze.

Where else would a Chinese new year carnival
5   puppet bang his glittery antennae on the mirrored catwalk to the sounds of house music and wild applause? Where else would ballet dancers in cherub-printed turquoise chiffon gowns, crystal lace sleeves and khaki army hats
10   parade clothes *en point*? And where else would the designer himself appear to take a standing ovation topless, in matador trousers and a comedy moustache? Even more perplexing than the clothes is the fact that Galliano's increasingly
15   incomprehensible designs for Christian Dior are being rewarded by commercial success at the company. By embracing the notion of fashion as fantasy, Galliano once more has women dreaming of Dior.

20   The show had begun with an air of disappointment. Contrary to rumour Britney Spears, currently in Paris, failed to appear in the front row, promising instead to attend the evening's Bride of the Vampire ball at the Paris
25   Ritz in honour of Dior's new jewellery collection.

Galliano's *modus operandi* appears to go something like this: imagine a woman in the most outlandish situation possible, and then dream up clothes that would be ridiculously
30   inappropriate even then. How about a coat with native American style embroidery and floor-length, gold-tasselled sleeves, a suede miniskirt, voluptuous fur boots? Oh, and do not forget the marigold coloured sheepskin headdress.

35   Between bouts of pure spectacle – somersaulting gymnasts in hooded lace tutus and kaleidoscopic ribbon bodices – there were a few dresses, if you looked carefully.

A long column dress, hourglass tight to the
40   knee and then flared to the floor, was elegant in velvety shades of mushroom, beige and silver; another gown, in coffee and cream polka dot chiffon, boasted Galliano's trademark spiral construction.

Evening coats, inch thick with embroidered sunflowers or boasting leopardskin epaulettes, also 45 strayed closer to reality, albeit the red-carpet kind.

When the lights came up – after a five-minute glitter storm and swirls of green dry ice – Gwyneth Paltrow, front row in jeans and T-shirt, looked dazzled and decidedly underdressed. 50

Activity 6

1 Scan the newspaper article on page 43 to find the answers to these questions:
   a What were the ballet dancers wearing?
   b Was Britney Spears at the show?
   c What gown boasted Galliano's trademark spiral construction?

2 Read the text closely and make notes on what it shows about attitudes to fashion.

3 Use your notes to write a paragraph explaining what you learn about different attitudes to fashion from this article and **Text D** on page 39.

Activity 7

Compare the article on the previous page with **Text B** on page 37. Focus on:
• purpose and audience (why each text was written and its intended reader)
• presentation (the way print and pictures are used)
• content (what each text is about).

Use the example on page 42 as a model for your writing.

POINTS TO REMEMBER

❗ We identify different types of text by their *appearance*.

❗ We *skim* a text to get a general idea of what it is about.

❗ We *scan* a text to find a particular detail.

❗ To *collate information* you take details from different texts and use them together.

❗ *Notes* should be adapted to the purpose for which they are required.

❗ To *compare texts* you need to point out the similarities and differences between them.

5 Reading with insight

Understanding meaning

One of the first things you do when you read something is to work out what it is about.

Activity **1**

To show your understanding of the following text you are going to write a summary of it. A summary is a brief account, which gives the main points of something. Your summary of the text will be no more than 100 words.

To help you with your summary, follow these steps:

Step 1 Read the text closely. As you read make a note of the key points, for example:

Captain Scott's diary
16–17 March Titus Oates couldn't go on – v. brave – went into blizzard – never returned

Step 2 Use your notes on the key points to help you answer these questions:

- What happens?
- Who does it happen to?
- Where does it happen?
- Why does it happen?
- When does it happen?

Step 3 Look at your answers to the questions. Have you enough information here to give someone who hasn't read the text an accurate account of what it is about? Are there any essential details missing? If so, add them to your answers.

Step 4 Write your summary. Your aims are:

- to show you have understood the text
- to give a brief account of the main points.

Remember to write your summary in no more than 100 words.

South Polar Expedition

On the 18th January, 1912, Captain Scott reached the South Pole, only to find that Roald Amundsen had got there about a month before. Scott and his companions never returned. On 17th November searchers found the tent with their frozen bodies and Scott's last diary.

Friday, March 16 or Saturday, 17. — Lost track of dates, but think the last correct. Tragedy all along the line. At lunch, the day before yesterday, poor Titus Oates said he couldn't go on; he proposed we should leave him in his sleeping-bag. That we could not do, and we induced him to come on, on the afternoon march. In spite of its awful nature for him he struggled on and we made a few miles. At night he was worse and we knew the end had come.

Should this be found I want these facts recorded. Oates' last thoughts were of his Mother, but immediately before he took pride in thinking that his regiment would be pleased with the bold way in which he met his death. We can testify to his bravery. He has borne intense suffering for weeks without complaint, and till the very last was able and willing to discuss outside subjects. He did not – would not – give up hope till the very end. He was a brave soul. This was the end. He slept through the night before last, hoping not to wake; but he woke in the morning – yesterday. It was blowing a blizzard. He said, 'I am just going outside and may be some time.' He went out into the blizzard and we have not seen him since.

I take this opportunity of saying that we have stuck to our sick companions to the last. In case of Edgar Evans, when absolutely out of food and he lay insensible, the safety of the remainder seemed to demand his abandonment, but Providence mercifully removed him at this critical moment. He died a natural death, and we did not leave him till two hours after his death. We knew that poor Oates was walking to his death, but though we tried to dissuade him, we knew it was the act of a brave man and an English gentleman. We all hope to meet the end with a similar spirit, and assuredly the end is not too far …

Sunday, March 18. — To-day, lunch, we are 21 miles from the depot. Ill fortune presses, but better may come. We have had more wind and drift from ahead yesterday; had to stop marching; wind N.W., force 4, temp. −35°. No human being could face it, and we are worn out nearly.

My right foot has gone, nearly all the toes – two days ago I was proud possessor of best feet. These are the steps of my downfall. Like an ass I mixed a small spoonful of curry powder with my melted pemmican – it gave me violent indigestion. I lay awake and in pain all night; woke and felt done on the march; foot went and I didn't know it. A very small measure of neglect and have a foot which is not pleasant to contemplate. Bowers takes first place in condition, but there is not much to choose after all. The others are still confident of getting through – or pretend to be – I don't know! We have the last half fill of oil in our primus and a very small quantity of spirit – this alone between us and thirst. The wind is fair for the moment, and that is perhaps a fact to help. The mileage would have seemed ridiculously small on our outward journey.

Monday, March 19. — Lunch. We camped with difficulty last night, and were dreadfully cold till after our supper of cold pemmican and biscuit and a half a pannikin of cocoa cooked over the spirit. Then, contrary to expectation, we got warm and all slept well. To-day we started in the usual dragging manner. Sledge dreadfully heavy. We are 15½ miles from the depot and ought to get there in three days. What progress! We have two days' food but barely a day's fuel. All our feet are getting bad – Wilson's best, my right foot worse, left all right. There is no chance to nurse one's feet till we can get hot food into us. Amputation is the least I can hope for now, but will the trouble spread? That is the serious question. The weather doesn't give us a chance – the wind from N. to N.W. and −40° temp. today.

Wednesday, March 21. — Got within 11 miles of depot on Monday night; had to lay up all yesterday in severe blizzard. To-day forlorn hope, Wilson and Bowers going to depot for fuel.

Thursday, March 22 and 23. — Blizzard bad as ever – Wilson and Bowers unable to start – to-morrow last chance – no fuel and only one or two of food left – must be near the end. Have decided it shall be natural – we shall march for the depot with or without our effects and die in our tracks.

Thursday, March 29. — Since the 21st we have had a continuous gale from W.S.W. and S.W. We had fuel to make two cups of tea apiece and bare food for two days on the 20th. Every day we have been ready to start for our depot 11 miles away, but outside the door of the tent it remains a scene of swirling drift. I do not think we can hope for any better things now. We shall stick it out to the end, but we are getting weaker, of course, and the end cannot be far.

It seems a pity, but I do not think I can write more —

Scott's Last Expedition,
by Captain Robert Scott

Referring to the text

When *answering questions* on a text you need to do more than demonstrate your understanding of it. You need to support the things you say in your answers with evidence from the text. This can be done by reference to a detail or by use of quotation.

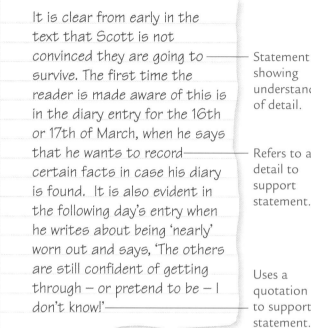

It is clear from early in the text that Scott is not convinced they are going to survive. The first time the reader is made aware of this is in the diary entry for the 16th or 17th of March, when he says that he wants to record certain facts in case his diary is found. It is also evident in the following day's entry when he writes about being 'nearly' worn out and says, 'The others are still confident of getting through – or pretend to be – I don't know!'

Statement showing understanding of detail.

Refers to a detail to support statement.

Uses a quotation to support statement.

Activity 2

Find and use evidence from the passage, by reference to detail or quotation, to support these statements:

- Titus Oates died bravely.
- Scott is suffering from frostbite.
- The men are travelling very slowly.
- They are prevented from reaching the depot by very bad weather.

Commenting on detail

When writing about a text you also need to comment on what you have read. Your comment might explain a point in more detail or express an opinion on a particular incident or character.

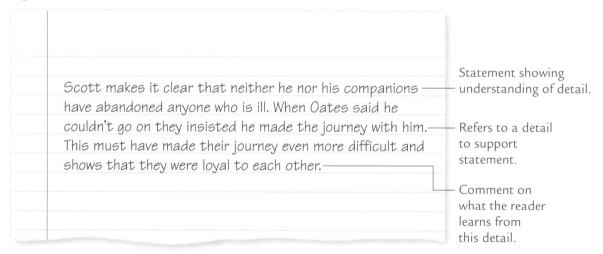

Scott makes it clear that neither he nor his companions have abandoned anyone who is ill. When Oates said he couldn't go on they insisted he made the journey with him. This must have made their journey even more difficult and shows that they were loyal to each other.

Statement showing understanding of detail.

Refers to a detail to support statement.

Comment on what the reader learns from this detail.

The ability to comment shows that you can make judgements based on the details of a text. It shows that you are thinking about what you read.

Complete the following chart by:
- finding evidence to support the statements
- developing your ideas into a comment.

Statement	Evidence	Comment
Scott makes it clear that neither he nor his companions have abandoned anyone who is ill.	When Oates said he couldn't go on they insisted he made the journey with him.	This must have made their journey even more difficult and shows that they were loyal to each other.
Oates was not the first to die.		
They have very little food left.		
They don't have far to go to reach the depot.		

Reading with insight

You show high-level reading skills when you:
- empathise by sharing another person's feelings
- infer meaning based on certain evidence
- make insightful comments on what you have read
- are sensitive to tone.

Empathy – I can imagine just how he feels …

Inference – That seems to suggest that …

Insight – Perhaps the writer wants us to think about …

Tone – It sounds as though he's feeling …

In the following sample answer a student demonstrates these skills.
Read the two paragraphs and look at the annotations carefully:

This must have been a terrible way to die, knowing that the depot was so close and that they just couldn't reach it. You can sense the despair in Scott's voice at certain times, particularly when, after Oates's death he writes, 'We all hope to meet the end with a similar spirit, and assuredly the end is not too far'. It's as though he accepted long before the others that they didn't have a chance but he still refused to give in and kept on trying for the sake of the others.

There is a helplessness but also a certain dignity in the understatement of the final line, 'It seems a pity ...' The last week must have been dreadful for all of them as they fought frostbite and starvation, unable to leave the shelter and knowing that they were getting closer to death. Perhaps what is most revealing is what Scott doesn't write in his diary. He hides the real awfulness of those last days, maybe through consideration for the relatives and friends who might read his diary at a later date. There is no sign of the anger, frustration and sadness he must have been feeling. Like Oates, he was a gentleman to the end.

- Empathises with the situation
- Shows sensitivity to tone
- Provides evidence to support comment
- Inference based on details in the text
- Shows sensitivity to tone
- Empathises with the situation
- Comments show insight and the ability to think beyond the text

Activity 4

Find these words in the extract from Captain Scott's diary and re-read the sentences in which they appear:

'Have decided it shall be natural ...'

'We shall stick it out to the end ...'

Discuss these lines and decide:

- what they show you about the way the men are thinking
- what they suggest about the kind of men these were
- whether, in the same situation, you would make the same decision.

Write a few sentences, showing what these lines reveal to you. Aim to show *inference*, *empathy* and *insight*.

Practice

Read the following passage. It is an *autobiographical* account, narrated in the first person by the writer, Joe Simpson.

Whilst climbing in the Peruvian Andes he experienced a dreadful fall. Considered dead by his fellow climber, he here describes his thoughts and feelings on waking the next morning.

I opened my eyes and flinched at the sharp glare of sunlight. Tears brimmed and watered my vision. I closed my eyes and made a mental check on myself. Cold and weak. It was still early and the sun had no warmth. Sharp stones pressed through the sodden fabric of my sleeping 5 bag. My neck ached. I had slept with my head crooked over between two rocks. The night had taken forever to pass. There had been little sleep. The hammering falls had severely affected my leg so that spasms of pain kept disturbing me when I dozed off. Once I had howled in agony when cramps in my thigh and calf muscles forced me to twist violently and bend forward 10 to massage the injured leg. When the pain throbbed too insistently for sleep, I had lain shivering on the rocky cleft where I had collapsed and stared at the night sky. Shooting-stars flared in the myriad bands of stars spread across the night. I watched them flare and die without interest. As the hours passed, the feeling that I would never get up overwhelmed me. I 15 lay unmoving on my back, feeling pinned to the rocks, weighed down by a numb weariness and fear until it seemed that the star-spread blackness above me was pushing me relentlessly into the ground. I spent so much of the night wide-eyed, staring at the timeless vista of stars, that time seemed frozen and spoke volumes to me of solitude and loneliness, leaving me with 20 the inescapable thought that I would never move again. I fancied myself lying there for centuries, waiting for a sun that would never rise. I slept in sudden stolen minutes and awoke to the same stars and the same inevitable thoughts. They talked to me without my consent, whispering dreads that I knew were untrue but couldn't ignore. The *voice* told me I 25 was too late; time had run out.

Now my head was basked in sunshine while my body lay shadowed by a large boulder on my left. I pulled the draw-cord open with my teeth and tried to shuffle out of the bag and into the sun. Every movement caused flares of pain in my knee. Though I moved only six feet, the effort left me slumped in 30 exhaustion on the screes. I could hardly believe how badly I had deteriorated during the night. Pulling myself along with my arms had become the limit of my strength. I shook my head from side to side, trying to wake myself and drive the lethargy away. It had no effect, and I lay back on the rocks. I had hit some sort of wall. I wasn't sure whether it was mental 35 or physical but it smothered me in a blanket of weakness and apathy. I wanted to move but couldn't. Lifting my arm to shield the sun from my eyes required a deliberate struggle. I lay motionless, frightened by my weakness. If I could get water I would have a chance. It would be just one chance. If I didn't reach the camp that day then I would never do so.

Touching the Void by Joe Simpson

1 Copy and complete the following chart to show:
   - your understanding of the account
   - your ability to refer to the text
   - your ability to comment on detail.

Content	My understanding	My evidence	My comment
Where the writer is			
What has happened to him			
What he has to do			

2 Re-read the extract from **Touching the Void**.
   a List the words and phrases in the extract that show you:
   - how the writer feels physically
   - the range of emotions he feels.
   Explain why he feels as he does.
   b What is the difference in tone between these lines:
   The *voice* told me I was too late; time had run out. (lines 24–5)
   If I could get water I would have a chance. (line 38)

3 Write an answer to this question:
   How does the writer feel during the night and in the early morning?
   Write two paragraphs. Aim to show:
   - understanding of the situation
   - empathy with the writer's feelings
   - sensitivity to tone.

POINTS TO REMEMBER

When answering questions on any text, you need to:
! show that you *understand* it
! support your points with *evidence*
! *comment* through explanation or opinion
! be *sensitive to tone*
! *empathise* with characters and situations
! *infer* meaning and make insightful comments.

How to approach Paper 1 Section A

Reading non-fiction and media texts

Now that you have developed the skills you need for Paper 1 Section A, you can start to look at the types of texts and questions you might come across in your examination. You will probably have two or perhaps three texts to read, one of which will be non-fiction and one media. These could include adverts, leaflets, news articles, extracts from diaries, autobiographies, biographies and travel writing. Aim to be familiar with materials of this kind *before* the exam.

Answering the questions

You are advised to spend **one hour** on Section A. Start by spending about ten minutes reading through the questions and the texts. The questions are placed at the beginning of the section in the examination paper so that you know what you have to do before you read the texts.

As you read, note key words, key points and line numbers, if relevant. This will:

- save you time later
- help you to avoid giving irrelevant details in your answers.

On the following pages you will find two Section A practice papers, one for Foundation Tier and one for Higher Tier. These papers are similar to the ones you can expect in the exam. Your teacher will tell you which one you should work on.

Each section is followed by a breakdown of the questions and advice on how you should answer them. You can **either** work through this advice carefully before you write your answers **or** use it to check that your answers are accurate.

Paper 1 Section A: Reading

Answer **all** the questions in this Section.

Spend about **60 minutes** on this Section.

Read the non-fiction text, **Famine in Ethiopia** and the media text, **Thinking of sponsoring a child**?

1 List three facts that are used to support the appeal in the leaflet, **Thinking of sponsoring a child?**

   Explain how each fact supports the appeal.   **(6 marks)**

2 **a** What images have shocked the writer of *Famine in Ethiopia*?   **(2 marks)**
   b Why does he find it so terrible that something like this could happen?   **(3 marks)**

3 **Thinking of sponsoring a child?** is a media text. Write about:
   - what you have found out about its intended purpose and audience
   - the way meaning is put across by the pictures it uses
   - how layout and presentation contribute to its effect.   **(9 marks)**

4 Think about the language of both texts. Which one is more likely to make you want to give money to help? Write about:
   - the ways the writers use language to persuade you
   - the effect the language has on you.   **(7 marks)**

Famine in Ethiopia

The news report was of famine in Ethiopia. From the first seconds it was clear that this was a horror on a monumental scale. The pictures were of people who were so shrunken by starvation that they looked like beings from another planet. Their arms and legs were as thin as
5 sticks, their bodies spindly. Their eyes looked into mine. There was a woman too weak to do anything but limply hold her dying child. There was a skeletal man holding out a bundle wrapped in sacking so that it could be counted; it looked like a tightly wrapped package of old sticks, but it was the body of his child. And there were children, their bodies
10 fragile and vulnerable as premature babies but with the consciousness of what was happening to them gleaming dully from their eyes. All around was the murmur of death, like a hoarse whisper, or the buzzing of flies.

The images played and replayed in my mind. What could I do? I could
15 send some money. Of course I could send some money. But that didn't seem enough. Did not the sheer scale of the whole thing call for something more?

There was something terrible about the idea that 2,000 years after Christ, in a world of modern technology something like this could be
20 allowed to happen as if the ability of mankind to influence and control the environment had not altered one jot. A horror like this could not occur today without our consent. We had allowed this to happen and now we knew that it was happening, to allow it to continue would be like murder. I would send some money, I would send more money. But
25 that was not enough.

1

Is That It? by Bob Geldof

Thinking of sponsoring a child?

Read how for just a small monthly amount you can bring health and opportunity to a child in a poor community

Plan
Be a part of it.

See what other Plan sponsors have to say

"When we first began sponsoring Orm-Jai, she was severely underweight for a two-year-old. Now she is a healthy eight-year-old who has clean drinking water, a proper latrine and, for the first time electricity in her village."

Jean and Ken McRonald, Dundee

"The personal link is very important to me, but more than that, regular updates keep me informed about improvements that are really being made."

Dr Lockyer, Aberdeenshire

Plan
Be a part of it.

Registered Office: Plan International UK
5-6 Underhill Street, London NW1 7HS
Tel: 020 7485 6612 Fax: 020 7485 2107
Website: www.plan-international.org.uk
Registered Charity No. 276035

The pictures in this leaflet are for representation purposes only. Names have been changed for reasons of confidentiality.

Every child has potential

There are 600 million children who live on less than 70p a day – that's more than ten times the UK population.

In Africa, Latin America and large areas of Asia, acute poverty is depriving children of good health. They are dying needlessly from malnutrition, and avoidable infections or diseases spread through contaminated water.

Their lack of education means they have little opportunity to learn skills which could help them find meaningful and long-term employment. Tragically, at a very early age, many have given up hope for a better future.

Without help today these children will never have the chances that can improve their lives. That's where you can help, by becoming a Plan child sponsor. As a Plan sponsor you can give a child, their family and whole community a better start in life.

With you as a sponsor a child can realise that potential

Children are at the heart of all Plan's work. We sponsor a million children across the world, that means we are helping ten million people. Because, for every one child sponsored, another nine people in that community benefit.

When we begin working with a community, the first thing we do is talk to community leaders, parents and the children themselves to find out what they need most.

It could be access to clean water, a school for both boys and girls, a medical centre so that mothers don't have to carry their sick babies to the nearest hospital, or an income generating scheme so that families can earn a living.

We start work immediately, but there are no simple solutions. Whatever help and practical support we do provide, it is long-lasting and will benefit the community for many years.

Children represent the future and we believe sponsorship is the best way to help communities. It is children like Trung, Mamadou and Amina who will be able to pass on their knowledge and skills to the next generation.

By becoming a Plan sponsor for £12 a month you can help children like them to create a better world.

Trung wants to read

An education will be the best start he can have in life. But Trung's parents cannot afford to send him to school.

Mamadou's family needs seeds

Mamadou and his family have a field that could provide food for them but they need seeds, plus advice to help them work their land more effectively.

Amina needs clean water

Amina's village only has access to dirty water, so many children's lives are threatened by waterborne illnesses such as dysentery and diarrhoea.

The examiner comments . . .

> **1** List three facts that are used to support the appeal in the leaflet, **Thinking of sponsoring a child?**
>
> Explain how each fact supports the appeal. **(6 marks)**

This question is testing you on your ability to *distinguish fact and opinion*.

It is worth 6 marks so it is likely you will gain 1 mark for each correct fact and 1 mark for each correct explanation.

Remember: facts can be proved to be true.

One fact you could select is that in Africa, Latin America and large areas of Asia, acute poverty is depriving children of good health.

Your explanation would be that this appeal is seeking to raise sponsorship and this fact makes the reader aware of how serious the problem is.

Now find two more facts *and* explain how each one supports the appeal.

> **2 a** What images have shocked the writer of *Famine in Ethiopia*? **(2 marks)**
>
> **b** Why does he find it so terrible that something like this could happen? **(3 marks)**

This question is asking you to show your understanding and that you can *follow an argument*.

In the first paragraph the writer shows that something terrible has happened when he describes the shocking scenes shown in the news report. In the second paragraph and third paragraph he develops the argument.

Re-read the second and third paragraphs and, **in your own words** explain the points he is making. Do not copy from the text. By using your own words you can show that you have understood the argument.

> **3 Thinking of sponsoring a child?** is a media text. Write about:
> - what you have found out about its intended purpose
> - what you have found out about its intended audience
> - the way meaning is put across by the pictures it uses
> - how the layout and presentation contribute to its effect. **(9 marks)**

This question tests both your understanding of, and your ability to evaluate, *how writers use structural and presentational devices*. Each bullet point is likely to be worth three marks:

Remember: *purpose* refers to why something is written and *audience* refers to the intended reader. Work out what the leaflet is trying to achieve and who it is written for. Show your examiner how you have worked this out.

To answer this, you need to think about how the pictures connect with or reflect the writing. Write about what the pictures show you and how they link with the written text.

You need to write about how the text is organised on the page, the presentational devices that are used and what they both contribute to the effectiveness of the leaflet.

---

4 Think about the language of both texts. Which one is more likely to make you want to give money to help? Write about:
  ● the ways the writers use language to persuade you
  ● the effect the language has on you.   (7 marks)

To answer this question you need to:
● *collate material* from both texts
● write about how writers use *linguistic devices*
● *show engagement* when discussing the ways the language affects you
● make sure you answer the question about which is the more likely to *persuade*.

If you look at the language of both texts you will find that it is used to describe, to argue and to persuade. Write about examples of different kinds of writing from the two texts. Use quotations from the texts to help you make your points clearly.

Remember to show how both writers use language emotively in order to make the readers feel something. Give examples of how both writers do this, what they are trying to make their readers feel, and how successful you think they are in doing this.

In order to answer the second bullet point in the question, you need to write about the way you are affected by the language of **both** texts. Again, you could choose particular examples to show which text has the most effect on you.

Exam Practice Higher Tier

Paper 1 Section A: Reading

Answer **all** the questions in this Section.

Spend about **60 minutes** on this Section.

Read the non-fiction text, **Famine in Ethiopia** and the media text, **Thinking of sponsoring a child**?

1 How is a range of factual evidence used to support the appeal in
Thinking of sponsoring a child?   (5 marks)

2 Why does the writer of **Famine in Ethiopia** find it so terrible that
something like this could happen? What evidence does he use to support
his point of view?   (5 marks)

3 **Thinking of sponsoring a child?** is a media text. What have you found out about:
   • its intended purpose and audience
   • how meaning is conveyed through pictures
   • how layout and presentation contribute to its effect?   (9 marks)

4 Which of the two texts would be more likely to persuade you to give money
to help? Compare:
   • their content and the ways the writers use language
   • the effect they have on you.   (8 marks)

Famine in Ethiopia

The news report was of famine in Ethiopia. From the first seconds it was clear that this was a horror on a monumental scale. The pictures were of people who were so shrunken by starvation that they looked like beings from another planet. Their arms and legs were as thin as sticks, their bodies spindly. Swollen
5 veins and huge, blankly staring eyes protruded from their shrivelled heads. The camera wandered amidst them like a mesmerised observer, occasionally dwelling on one person so that he looked directly at me, sitting in my comfortable living room surrounded by the fripperies of modern living which we were pleased to regard as necessities. Their eyes looked into mine. There
10 was an emaciated woman too weak to do anything but limply hold her dying child. There was a skeletal man holding out a bundle wrapped in sacking so that it could be counted; it looked like a tightly wrapped package of old sticks, but it was the desiccated body of his child. And there were children, their bodies fragile and vulnerable as premature babies but with the consciousness of what
15 was happening to them gleaming dully from their eyes. All around was the murmur of death, like a hoarse whisper, or the buzzing of flies.

Right from the first few seconds it was clear that this was a tragedy which the world had somehow contrived not to notice until it had reached a scale which constituted an international scandal. You could hear that in the tones of
20 the reporter. It was not the usual dispassionate objectivity of the BBC. It was the voice of a man who was registering despair, grief and absolute disgust at what he was seeing.

That night I could not sleep. I returned to the old sleep-inducing formula I had employed so successfully at school. I would imagine myself spinning ever
25 faster towards a point of pure white light in a black void. As I reached maximum velocity, I would reach the light and fall fast asleep. But this time the point of light was an image from the news report. There were tens of thousands of people in the camp in Ethiopia where it had been filmed and where a handful of European aid workers were distributing a pitiful amount of food. One young
30 nurse had the awesome task of selecting the few hundred individuals who were to be fed. They sat inside a compound enclosed by a low wall and waited for the food. Outside thousands of their fellows stood and watched. They had

Is That It?
by Bob Geldof

been condemned to death and now they stood to watch the few who had been offered a small chance of immediate survival. There was no anger in their faces,
35 no bitterness, no clamouring. There was only the hollow dignity of waiting for death in silence.

The image played and replayed in my mind. What could I do? I could send some money. Of course I could send some money. But that didn't seem enough. Did not the sheer scale of the whole thing call for something more?
40 There was something terrible about the idea that 2,000 years after Christ, in a world of modern technology something like this could be allowed to happen as if the ability of mankind to influence and control the environment had not altered one jot. A horror like this could not occur today without our consent. We had allowed this to happen and now we knew that it was happening, to
45 allow it to continue would be like murder. I would send some money, I would send more money. But that was not enough.

Thinking of sponsoring a child?

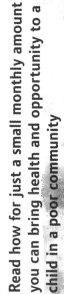

Read how for just a small monthly amount you can bring health and opportunity to a child in a poor community

Plan
Be a part of it.

Michael Aspel answers your questions

Michael Aspel is a Plan sponsor and patron

Q. Can my help really make a difference?
A. The proof is in the thousands of schools, clinics and wells that Plan have helped provide, plus the many income-generating projects they've helped families to start.

Q. How can I be sure my money is well spent?
A. On average, approximately 80p of every £1 contributed goes towards our development work. Your money will benefit Plan's work world-wide. An annual report from our local field office will show you what you have helped to achieve.

Q. Can I choose my sponsored child?
A. You can choose to sponsor either a girl or boy from a community that Plan are already working in.

Q. Will I hear from my child?
A. Some children love writing and send several letters a year but others are less communicative. Plan's field staff will make sure you receive news of your child at least once a year.

Q. How long should I continue to be a sponsor?
A. Children are normally sponsored until they reach the age of 18 but you can withdraw at any time.

Plan have 65 years experience as a child sponsorship organisation, working to promote the rights of children in 57 countries. We are a non-religious, non-political organisation that works with local communities to implement vital projects to improve the quality of life for children and their families across the developing world.

See what other Plan sponsors have to say

"When we first began sponsoring Orm-Jai, she was severely underweight for a two-year-old. Now she is a healthy eight-year-old who has clean drinking water, a proper latrine and, for the first time electricity in her village."

Jean and Ken McRonald, Dundee

"The personal link is very important to me, but more than that, regular updates keep me informed about improvements that are really being made."

Dr Lockyer, Aberdeenshire

Plan
Be a part of it.

Registered Office: Plan International UK
5-6 Underhill Street, London NW1 7HS
Tel: 020 7485 6612 Fax: 020 7485 2107
Website: www.plan-international.org.uk
Registered Charity No 276035

The pictures in this leaflet are for representation purposes only.
Names have been changed for reasons of confidentiality.

Every child has potential

There are 600 million children who live on less than 70p a day – that's more than ten times the UK population.

In Africa, Latin America and large areas of Asia, acute poverty is depriving children of good health. They are dying needlessly from malnutrition, and avoidable infections or diseases spread through contaminated water.

Their lack of education means they have little opportunity to learn skills which could help them find meaningful and long-term employment. Tragically, at a very early age, many have given up hope for a better future.

Without help today these children will never have the chances that can improve their lives. That's where you can help, by becoming a Plan child sponsor. As a Plan sponsor you can give a child, their family and whole community a better start in life.

With you as a sponsor a child can realise that potential

Children are at the heart of all Plan's work. We sponsor a million children across the world, that means we are helping ten million people. Because, for every one child sponsored, another nine people in that community benefit.

When we begin working with a community, the first thing we do is talk to community leaders, parents and the children themselves to find out what they need most.

It could be access to clean water, a school for both boys and girls, a medical centre so that mothers don't have to carry their sick babies to the nearest hospital, or an income generating scheme so that families can earn a living.

We start work immediately, but there are no simple solutions. Whatever help and practical support we do provide, it is long-lasting and will benefit the community for many years.

Children represent the future and we believe sponsorship is the best way to help communities. It is children like Trung, Mamadou and Amina who will be able to pass on their knowledge and skills to the next generation.

By becoming a Plan sponsor for £12 a month you can help children like them to create a better world.

Sponsorship helps build strong communities for the future

When you sponsor a child with Plan you benefit a family and an entire community. With over 65 years experience, we know that a child can only develop in a thriving community that has skills and resources which bring self-sufficiency and dignity. Our ultimate goal is to leave the community because they no longer need Plan's help.

Share the successes, become a Plan sponsor today

Sponsorship is real people helping real people. It costs just £12 a month and gives you an insight into a culture very different from your own.

Plan is an accountable charity, so sponsors receive regular progress reports from field officers. As well as showing you how your contributions are being spent, they keep you up-to-date with projects you have helped Plan to achieve, so you can see the difference you are making. As well as the successes, we'll also tell you about any setbacks.

Many sponsors exchange letters with their sponsored child to help build up a strong personal relationship over the years.

Help a child in need by completing the sponsorship form and becoming a sponsor.

Please call 020 7485 6612 for more details or visit the Plan website www.plan-international.org.uk

Trung wants to read

An education will be the best start he can have in life. But Trung's parents cannot afford to send him to school.

Mamadou's family needs seeds

Mamadou and his family have a field that could provide food for them but they need seeds, plus advice to help them work their land more effectively.

Amina needs clean water

Amina's village only has access to dirty water, so many children's lives are threatened by waterborne illnesses such as dysentery and diarrhoea.

The examiner comments . . .

The Foundation and Higher Tiers often have one text in common. The leaflet **Thinking of sponsoring a child?** appears on both tiers. The second text may be completely different or may, as in this case, be taken from the same source. Here, it is the longer, unedited version of **Famine in Ethiopia**.

The questions, whilst usually focusing on the same Assessment Objectives, are more difficult at the Higher Tier. They are worded differently and usually give fewer clues as to how they should be answered.

The distribution of marks may, as in this case, differ from Foundation Tier.

---

1 How is a range of factual evidence used to support the appeal in **Thinking of sponsoring a child?** (5 marks)

This question is testing you on your ability to *distinguish fact and opinion*. You are being asked to select a range of facts and to show how they are used to support the appeal. To show the range you need to select facts from different sections of the leaflet. You could start by using the fact that in Africa, Latin America and large areas of Asia acute poverty is depriving children of good health.

Your explanation would be that this appeal is seeking to raise sponsorship and this fact makes the reader aware of how serious the problem is.

Now find three or four other facts from different sections of the leaflet and show how **each** one supports the appeal.

---

2 Why does the writer of **Famine in Ethiopia** find it so terrible that something like this could happen? What evidence does he use to support his point of view? (5 marks)

This question is asking you to show that you can *follow an argument* and *select detail appropriate to purpose*. You need to examine how the argument is built. You should start with the vivid description of the shocking scenes shown in the news report and how these are contrasted with the modern western lifestyle. Then find other evidence that suggests this is something terrible and unacceptable.

The argument is summarised in the final paragraph and you need to show that you have understood this. Use your own words, not the writer's, to do so.

---

3 Thinking of sponsoring a child? is a media text. What have you found out about:
- its intended purpose and audience
- how meaning is conveyed through pictures
- how layout and presentation contribute to its effect? (9 marks)

This question tests both your understanding of, and your ability to evaluate, how writers use *structural and presentational devices*. Each bullet point is likely to be worth three marks:

Remember: *purpose* refers to why something is written **and** *audience* refers to the intended reader. Work out what the leaflet is trying to achieve and who it is written for. Show your examiner how you have worked this out.

To answer this, you need to think about how the pictures connect with or reflect the writing. Write about what the pictures show you and how they link with the written text.

Finally, you need to write about how the text is organised on the page, the presentational devices that are used and what they both contribute to the effectiveness of the leaflet.

---

4 Which of the two texts would be more likely to persuade you to give money to help?

Compare the texts in terms of:
- their content and the ways the writers use language
- the effect they have on you. **(8 marks)**

To answer this question you need to:
- *collate material* from both texts
- write about *similarities* and *differences* between content and use of language
- *show engagement* when comparing the effects of the two texts
- make sure you answer the question about which is the more likely to *persuade*.

Aim to identify the ways in which the texts are:
- about similar things
- about different things.

Think about how language is used to *describe*, *argue* and *persuade*. Write about examples of different kinds of writing from the two texts. Remember to show how both writers use language emotively in order to make the readers feel something.

In order to answer the second bullet point you need to write about the way you are affected by both texts. Choose particular examples to explain why you find one text more effective than the other.

Section B: *Writing to Argue, Persuade or Advise*

In your exam you will be given a choice of writing tasks which require you to argue, persuade or advise. There may also be a further choice of tasks which combine some of these. The tasks may be linked to themes or topics of the materials in Section A of the paper.

You will be assessed on your ability in three areas:

Communication

You need to:

- state your ideas clearly and imaginatively
- adapt your writing for different purposes and readers
- be able to write in different forms, for example, a letter.

Organisation

You need to:

- organise your ideas into sentences, paragraphs and whole texts
- use a varied and appropriate vocabulary range and range of linguistic features
- use a variety of structural features, for example, a decisive conclusion.

Accuracy

You need to:

- use appropriate grammatical structures
- punctuate your writing accurately
- spell words correctly.

In the following pages we look at:

- examples of the different types of writing you will be asked to do
- the ways you should use the skills you have, and how to develop new skills.

1 Writing for purpose and audience

Purpose and audience

When you write something it has:

- a **purpose:** the reason(s) for which you are writing it
- an **audience:** an intended reader; the person (or people) for whom you are writing.

Activity 1

1 Use a chart like the one below to map out the *purpose* and *audience* of **five** writing tasks you have done in school over the last week. Some examples are given to get you started.

Task: What I had to write	Purpose	Intended audience
Geography: notes on volcanoes	• to record key points • to have notes for revision	• my teacher • me
English: alternative openings for a horror story	• to show I could create a spooky atmosphere • to read out to class	• my teacher • other pupils

Activity 2

Now look at the **Texts A–H** opposite, and for each one identify and note down the purpose and audience. Are there any where these are not clear? If so, what extra information do you need?

A

15th March

Not a good day today. Started badly and got worse...

B

LASTING BOND

**The Real James Bond,
Tuesday, C4**

The character he created, the suave, sophisticated, sexy superspy, is one of the world's best-known brands, but what do we really know about the author?

It's 40 years since the world premiere of Dr No, the first of Ian Fleming's Bond stories to be made into a film.

Now the programme examines the public image of the writer, and explores the troubled psyche which lurked beneath the veneer of the upper-class English gent who died in 1964, aged 56.

Ian Fleming (right) has always been associated with his hero James Bond, thanks to his wry, disarming smile, stylish ebony cigarette holder and his Naval Intelligence background.

But it seems the real Ian Fleming was deeply shy and insecure, and his relationships with women were often complex and emotionally destructive.

Fans of the author with a licence to kill will be intrigued by this insight into the man who started the 007 franchise.

C

VENICE SIMPLON
ORIENT-EXPRESS

DESTINATION

NAME
HOME ADDRESS

POST CODE

D

The Prime Minister will, today, face fury from the Opposition and some of his own Back Benchers when he reveals plans to...

E Darlington Arts Centre

Tutti-Frutti presents
Humpty goes...Splatt!

Humpty goes...
tutti frutti
SPLATT!

In life there are some things that are sensible and some that aren't. An egg sitting on a wall is not sensible. In fact, it's just asking for trouble!

Funny, engaging, occasionally wicked and slightly bonkers, Humpty goes...Splatt! is delicious theatre for adults...and anyone over the age of 3.

F 2 *The Guardian*

12.02.02

The two-minute Guardian

Pop dollar Dido, catapulted from obscurity to global success in a year, was reported to be Britian's highest earning female pop star **8**
Train tampering Around 40 illegal immigrants were on the run yesterday after tampering with the brakes on a freight train **12**
French election President Jacques Chirac has formally declared himself a candidate for re-election this spring **13**
War crimes The Bush administration is considering ways of putting a time limit on the work of the Hague tribunal on war crimes **16**

G

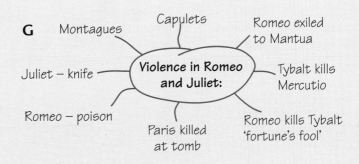

Montagues — Capulets — Romeo exiled to Mantua

Juliet – knife — **Violence in Romeo and Juliet:** — Tybalt kills Mercutio

Romeo – poison — Paris killed at tomb — Romeo kills Tybalt 'fortune's fool'

Writing for different audiences

It is important to think carefully about your audience before you start to write. Your audience will affect:

- what you include in your writing
- the way that you write.

Writing for a younger audience

When writing for very young children remember that:

- they have a limited vocabulary so words should be as simple as possible
- they have difficulty in handling different ideas at the same time so sentences should be short, easy to follow and contain one simple idea
- there should be a close link between ideas in separate sentences so that the child can follow the points that are being made.

Activity 4

Write your own piece for young children – about starting at primary school. Your *purpose* is to tell them what to expect. Adapt your writing to the needs of young children by:

- using mainly words with no more than two syllables
- keeping sentences short and easy to follow
- making clear links between sentences.

You should write about 100 words.

Activity 3

Read the following extract from a book for young children. Identify how the writer meets the needs of young children. You should focus on:

- the *information* that is given
- the *words* used
- *sentence structure* and *length*
- the *links* between the sentences.

BEING BORN and GROWING UP

apple pip poppy seed

Everything that a plant needs to help it to develop is contained within its seed. Look at the apple and the poppy seeds.

Protected by the earth the seeds develop shoots which grow towards the light. Seedlings appear.

The poppy only grows for a single season. The apple tree keeps on growing year after year.

The hen is keeping her eggs warm. Inside each egg a chick develops.

When the chicks are fully formed, they use their little beaks to break open the eggshells.

Some of the newly-hatched chicks will grow up to be cockerels and some will grow into hens.

After a month the chicks have grown crests on their heads. It is still hard to tell male from female.

Now the chicks have grown up to become a cockerel and a hen. Soon some eggs will be laid, and more chicks will be hatched.

The puppies are sucking milk from the mother dog's teats. Puppies develop and grow very quickly.

At four months a puppy is independent, playful and curious. When he grows up, he will get together with a female, called a bitch, and more puppies will be born.

Writing for older children

Older children, aged eight to eleven, have a much broader understanding of words and can grasp the meaning of quite complex sentences. Even so, they are not likely to be interested in material written for a teenage or adult audience.

As a writer, you have to work particularly hard to capture their imaginations and make them read on. Here is the introduction to a history book with a difference. Some of the features of the writing are annotated for you:

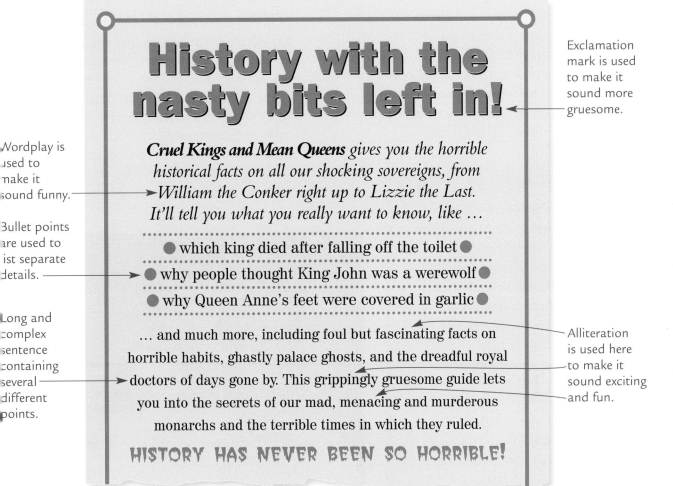

Exclamation mark is used to make it sound more gruesome.

History with the nasty bits left in!

Cruel Kings and Mean Queens gives you the horrible historical facts on all our shocking sovereigns, from William the Conker right up to Lizzie the Last. It'll tell you what you really want to know, like ...

- which king died after falling off the toilet
- why people thought King John was a werewolf
- why Queen Anne's feet were covered in garlic

... and much more, including foul but fascinating facts on horrible habits, ghastly palace ghosts, and the dreadful royal doctors of days gone by. This grippingly gruesome guide lets you into the secrets of our mad, menacing and murderous monarchs and the terrible times in which they ruled.

HISTORY HAS NEVER BEEN SO HORRIBLE!

Wordplay is used to make it sound funny.

Bullet points are used to list separate details.

Long and complex sentence containing several different points.

Alliteration is used here to make it sound exciting and fun.

Activity 5

Write a humorous passage for older children about to start secondary school. Your purpose is to warn them of the horrors of secondary school!

Adapt your writing to the needs of older children by using:

- a range of complex and simple words
- bullet points to organise detail
- some long, complex sentences
- alliteration and wordplay.

Writing for a teenage audience

Teenagers are often considered one of the most difficult audiences to write for. They want to be treated as adults and not talked down to. At the same time they often need reassurance and help.

The following text was written for fifteen and sixteen year olds and contains extracts from the prospectus of a sixth form college. Its purpose is to *inform* the audience **and** to *encourage* them to go to the college after GCSEs.

Activity 6

Look at the following incomplete statements. They focus on particular features of the text. Match them to the annotation numbers 1 to 7 and complete them by saying why the writer has used each feature:

a Uses formal adult vocab to …

b Addresses reader directly to …

c Deliberately does not refer to Mum and Dad to …

d Uses conversational, friendly tone to …

e Adopts student voice to …

f Uses questions to …

g Uses short sentence to …

How is college different to school?

1 → Well, there's no bells, no school uniform, no assemblies and first-name terms are used with teaching staff. You will be associating with lots of students the same age as you, and you are treated as an adult. College aims to provide you with a stepping stone between school and what you want to do next in life.

You get more free time to take responsibility for your own learning and self-development, but you are never on your own. There are plenty of staff around to help. Just ask. York College is also much bigger so there are more computers, more specialist equipment and many opportunities to play sport, pursue hobbies, try out new activities, see bands, meet people and have fun while learning.

The writer of this prospectus has tried to address the reader as an adult and offer reassuring answers to potential questions or concerns. Sometimes these ideas are placed next to each other as in the following examples:

> You get more free time to take responsibility for your own learning and self-development, but you are never on your own.
>
> The more work you do at college, the less you'll need to do at home!

This placing of different ideas next to each other is sometimes referred to as *juxtaposition*. Can you find another example of this in the text?

4

What are tutorials?

The purpose of the tutorial system is to help you get the most out of your time at college and to support your learning and overall well-being. It's our responsibility to make sure that you are doing justice to yourself in your studies, as well as making the most of the opportunities available to you.

5

Your development at college is regularly reviewed between yourself and your tutors, and then communicated to people at home via regular reports and progress evenings.

6

7

Will I get homework?

That depends on how well you use your time at college. We expect you to take more responsibility for your own learning than you may have been used to and to spend more time while at college working on assignments on your own or in small groups. The more work you do at college, the less you'll need to do at home!

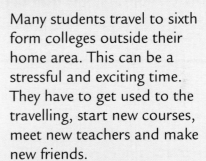

Activity 7

Many students travel to sixth form colleges outside their home area. This can be a stressful and exciting time. They have to get used to the travelling, start new courses, meet new teachers and make new friends.

Write the next page of this college brochure with these students in mind.

You should aim to include:
- the features you identified in Activity 6
- two examples of juxtaposition.

When you have completed your writing, highlight the features and examples you have used.

Adapting writing to purpose and audience

The age of your intended audience is an important factor, but there are other things you need to consider as well. The following texts were both written with the purpose of *persuading* adults to go on a particular holiday.

Activity 8

1 Read the following extracts from holiday brochures and make notes on:
   - The information given in each text. Think about:
     - things to do
     - places to go.
   - The way each text is written. Think about:
     - vocabulary
     - sentence length and structure
     - punctuation.

   Choose your own method for organising your notes.

2 Look back over your notes. What can you work out from them about the intended audiences of each of the two texts?

   Write a brief profile (two to three sentences) of the intended audience of each text. You could start with:

   The Corton brochure seems to be written for …

The type of writing found in holiday brochures often uses *noun phrases*. A noun phrase is a group of words which contains a noun and extra information about that noun which can affect the way the reader responds. They may be short, for example:

A fun atmosphere (Corton brochure)

They can also be extended, for example:

An impressive position high on a clifftop overlooking Suffolk's sandy beaches (Corton brochure)

Activity 9

1 Find and list five examples of noun phrases in the Bodrum Gumbet brochure.

2 What are the effects of the noun phrases you have listed?

Corton

If you're looking for a fun atmosphere, then **Corton** is the perfect choice, with enthusiastic staff ensuring your stay is complemented by friendly service at all times.

Corton enjoys an impressive position high on a clifftop overlooking Suffolk's sandy beaches – just one of the many reasons our guests come back to us time and time again.

But if socialising is more your style, no problem. Corton is renowned for its lively entertainment programme and popular themed breaks, incorporating music and dancing that are second to none. Popular attractions have included our acclaimed 'Summer Carnival Extravaganza' and the celebrated 'Golden Years of Variety'.

In between all the fun, take advantage of Corton's sports and leisure options – from swimming in our indoor pool to a game of bowls, boules, snooker or billiards. Or pit your wits against those of your fellow guests in one of our regular quizzes and pub games. It's a great way to meet and make friends with fellow guests. All this plus bars, a restaurant, shop and library make Corton the place to come if you want to enjoy the fun in a group as well as going off and doing your own thing when you feel like it.

What you get?

Not only do you get the up-front, thumping resorts of Bodrum and Gumbet oozing with bars and nightlife, but you also get a cosmopolitan resort which is a hardcore shoppers' paradise … tons of cheap gold, leather and fake designer stuff! The weather is great for all you sun-worshippers!

What's on?

All adventure days and nights try out Reps Cabaret, Sunkissed Cruise or the fabulous night cruise at Halikarnas. Get wet at one of the two water-parks and round it all off throwing shapes 'til the early hours! When you need to chill treat yourself to a session at Scrubbers Paradise (Turkish baths).

On the Beach

The main, man-made beach at Gumbet is where it's all at so consequently it gets very busy. Bodrum has a small pebble beach. Bars, cafés and shops surround both beaches.

Bars, Clubs & Music

If modern chart anthems and party tunes are your scene then Turkey is yours to be conquered! Halikarnas is a huge open-air club with a wicked laser show, £10 to get in. Choosing which bar to go to first will not be easy, especially when you've got bars such as Sensi, Red Lion, White House, Robin Hood, Temple, Central, Mystery and the Beach Club to choose from. You'll just have to go to them all!

Practice

1 Imagine you work for a holiday firm. You have been asked to write a one-paragraph insert for each of the three brochures, on the subjects listed in the chart below.

You will need to:

- write about the things most likely to appeal to your targeted audience
- adapt your language to suit your targeted audience
- use noun phrases for effect.

The third column of the chart gives you some ideas to get you started.

Subjects	Intended audience	Clues to help you
The swimming pool in a hotel suitable for families with young children.	Parents of young children	Exciting, adventurous, clean, safe, warm
The country surroundings of a cottage intended for the over-sixties.	The over-sixties	Peaceful, good for walking but not hilly; attractive, natural
The range of night-time activities for teenagers on a family campsite.	Teenagers and their parents	Lively, exciting, late, varied, friendly, trouble-free.

2 When you have finished writing your three inserts, write a commentary on one of them showing how you have targeted your audience through:

- the things you have written about
- the way you have written about it.

Your commentary should be about 100–150 words.

POINTS TO REMEMBER !

! Everything you write has a *purpose* and an *audience*.

! It is important to think carefully about your audience before starting to write.

! Your audience will affect what you write and the way you write.

! The placing of different ideas next to each other is sometimes referred to as *juxtaposition*.

Developing a point of view

One aim of *writing to argue* is to present and develop a particular point of view. In order to argue convincingly, you need to make a series of clear and logical points.

Read the following letter to a local newspaper in which the writer argues against using animal fur for clothing.

Activity 1

The following is a list of the key points made by the writer of the letter. Arrange them into the correct sequence as you read through the letter.

a conditions in mink farms are cramped and unpleasant

b luxurious fake furs are available

c both trapping and factory farming are vile

d conditions are also bad for caged foxes

e animals can be trapped in agony for days

f the trapped animal cannot escape

g ugly people wear fur

h one fur coat can cause the death of many animals

i some reptiles are skinned alive

Fur coat's high price

Some years ago, I was speaking to a self-professed animal lover, by whose calling (nursing) one would expect compassion to be second nature.

She was wearing a fur coat. When I expressed horror at this she protested, 'but I feel the cold so much. It'll be my last one!' She ignored the fact that, through her, it was the last of life itself for many animals, as just one coat can cause the death of 12 baby ocelots, or 15 lynx, or 40 foxes, or 65 mink, or 60 rabbits.

How can anyone presume to claim their warmth demands such a terrible sacrifice, especially when luxurious fake furs are available?

The two main forms of fur-bearing animal exploitation are trapping and factory-farming. Both methods are so vile, that one wonders how anyone can bear to wear the end 'product'.

Animals can be trapped, in excruciating agony, for days, before the trapper returns. The frantic, crazed-with-pain, creature in a trap, sometimes gnaws off the affected limb, to try to break free. Some animals (mainly foxes and otters) are so desperate, they shatter all their teeth on the steel traps, and their jawbones are raw and exposed.

The trapper is not willing to lose an animal which has amputated a limb, so what does he do? He fastens his traps to springy stakes which shoot up when the trap's jaws have snapped to, and the victim dangled (with no hope of escape) from one leg, until either its death or the return of the trapper.

Snakes, crocodiles and lizards are often skinned alive, and all for the sake of a hand-bag or shoes – a status symbol.

Farm factories are another evil. There, mink (which favour a solitary life, and space) are reared intensively, crammed two or three into a cage, which has a floor of thin wire mesh – the cages stretching in interminable rows, all exposed to winter's stormy blast, so the fur will grow faster.

Foxes, also, spend their lives shuffling backwards and forwards, in stereotyped fashion in small cages. Silver foxes are mated in February or March, and the cubs are born 51 days later, reared in cages and killed in their first winter.

There's not even a brief taste of the wild for these poor creatures.

A badge defines it all: 'Fur coats are worn by beautiful animals – and ugly people.'

How True!

Miss E. D. Irving, Park Avenue, Hexham

The writer uses a range of stylistic techniques to make her letter more interesting to the readers and to make her argument more convincing and more effective.

 Activity 2

1 The following chart identifies some of the *stylistic techniques* that appear in the letter, **Fur coat's high price**. Copy the chart and complete it by explaining why the writer has used each of these stylistic techniques.

Stylistic techniques	Example	What this achieves
Use of emotive language	'terrible sacrifice' 'excruciating agony' 'frantic, crazed-with-pain'	Invites the reader to respond emotionally by highlighting the suffering
Inclusion of facts	'...one coat can cause the death of 12 baby ocelots, or 15 lynx, or 40 foxes, or 65 mink, or 60 rabbits.'	
Use of rhetorical questions	'How can anyone presume to claim their warmth demands such a terrible sacrifice, especially when luxurious fake furs are available?'	
Use of personal anecdote	'Some years ago, I was speaking to...'	
Use of opinion	'Both methods are so vile, that one wonders how anyone can bear to wear the end "product".'	
Inclusion of examples	'Some animals (mainly foxes and otters) are so desperate, they shatter all their teeth on the steel traps ...'	

2 Find at least one more example of each of these stylistic techniques in the letter.

Sometimes writers, when explaining or developing an idea in a paragraph, will start with a *topic sentence*. This usually:

- provides a link with the previous paragraph
- clearly signals what the paragraph will be about.

Look at the opening sentence of the second paragraph:

'She' links to the 'self-professed animal lover' in the first paragraph.

She was wearing a fur coat.

In the rest of the paragraph the writer explores what it means to wear a fur coat.

Activity 3

Re-read lines 12 to 25. Copy the opening sentence of each of the three paragraphs. Highlight and annotate each one to show:

- how it links to the previous paragraph
- how it signals what the paragraph will be about.

Activity 4

Make a plan for the *content of a letter* on a subject you feel strongly about. You could choose one of the following:

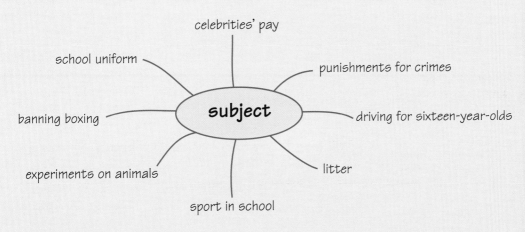

Your plan should include:

- your chosen subject
- key points
- anecdotal evidence
- facts
- opinions
- examples
- some topic sentences.

You can 'make up' your anecdotal evidence and your examples.
An examiner will not know they are made up, as long as they sound believable.

Writing letters to express a point of view

There are two main types of letter.

A Formal

This is the type of letter you might write when applying for a job or a place on a course, or to a newspaper to express a point of view.

There are many different ways of setting out formal letters and these are constantly changing, particularly with the increased use of word-processors. Nevertheless, some conventions remain unchanged and you need to follow these whenever you are required to write a formal letter.

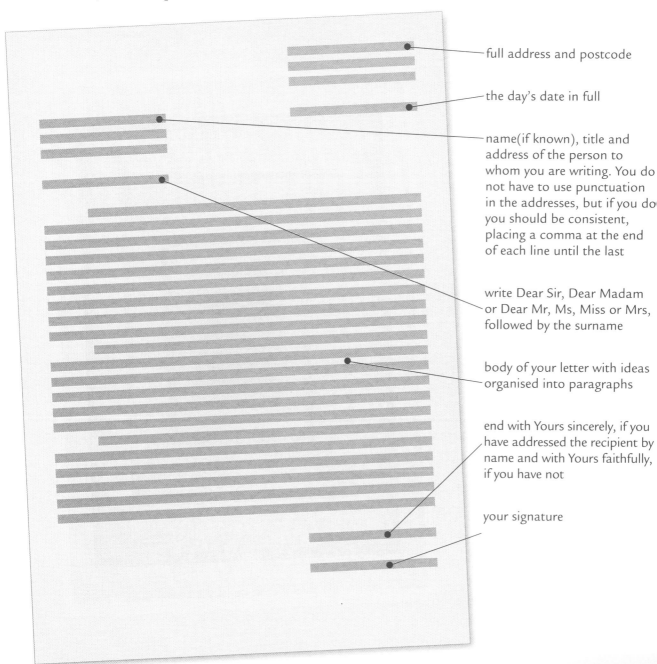

full address and postcode

the day's date in full

name(if known), title and address of the person to whom you are writing. You do not have to use punctuation in the addresses, but if you do you should be consistent, placing a comma at the end of each line until the last

write Dear Sir, Dear Madam or Dear Mr, Ms, Miss or Mrs, followed by the surname

body of your letter with ideas organised into paragraphs

end with Yours sincerely, if you have addressed the recipient by name and with Yours faithfully, if you have not

your signature

B Informal

This is the type of letter you might write to a friend or a relative to catch up on recent news. In an informal letter you still need to include your address and the date but not the name and address of the person to whom you are writing. You address the recipient by his or her first name or the name by which you usually call them, e.g. *Dear Ann, Dear Chris, Dear Gran*. An informal ending such as *Best wishes*, or *Love from*, is followed by your signature.

Getting the conventions of letter-writing right is only a small part of writing a good letter. It is what you say that is of most importance. A good letter should be clear, logically sequenced and appropriate to its purpose and audience.

In your English exam you are most likely to be asked to write a formal letter. This might be to a magazine, newspaper or an official body, such as the local council.

Activity 5

Look back at the plan of a letter you made in Activity 4.

Use this to help you write a letter to a local newspaper in which you present and develop your point of view on a subject you feel strongly about.

You should aim to:

- organise your content in a *logical order*
- include *rhetorical questions* and *use words emotively*
- follow the *conventions* of formal letter-writing.

Looking at both sides of the argument

Newspapers and magazines often contain articles based on *argument*. These can present and develop one point of view, as did the letter **Fur coat's high price**. Sometimes, however, they are less emotive and present a more balanced argument.

Activity 6

1 Read the following article closely. As you read, list the *key points* that the writer makes.

2 When you have finished reading the article, study the annotations and answer the questions they raise.

THE BELLS, THE BELLS

ROGER ST PIERRE gives audible warning of new ideas for canalside cyclists

1 Think about the title, the illustration and the opening paragraph. How are they used to create humour?

Ting-a-ling-a-ling! Time was when it was deemed obligatory to have a bell on your bike. That was before, somewhere in the Fifties and after a long fight, the cycling lobby managed to win their argument that a shouted warning of 'Oi! Get out of the way!' qualified as the Road Traffic Act's requisite 'audible warning of approach'.

Though manufacturers continued to supply a bell with each new bike they sold – somewhere separately in the cardboard bike box and usually destined to be thrown out with the wrappings – to all intents bicycle bells went the way of cycle clips.

The arguments had been cogent: that the human voice carries further than any bicycle bell – though not as far as an electrically powered horn! – and that, in any event, fingers grabbing for the bell would be better used grabbing for the brakes.

2 Use of first person plural: what does this allow the writer to do?

End of story … or so we thought. Now, however, several decades later there are people who would like cycle bell manufacturers to get back into business (I hope they'll produce those natty little numbers in glitzy anodised finishes rather than drab aluminium or plain chrome!)

It seems that walkers, anglers and everyman and his dog wants bikies to (a) be more considerate (fair enough) and (b) to unfailingly give warning of imminent approach (though I guess, before too long they'll be complaining just as stridently about being disturbed by all the resultant noise.

It seems that the British Waterways Board is looking at the possibility of charging – yes, charging – cyclists for the use of their towpaths. It's only an idea up for discussion and don't blame them for looking into it; Government pressure is now for all public bodies to maximise their income potential rather than being fully supported out of general taxation as was the case in the days when public service was regarded as a mission from God and not a dirty word.

The argument is that canal-boaters pay to glide along the waters and anglers pay to fish in them, so why shouldn't cyclists pay for the right to ride alongside them, especially since it is the board which has to upkeep the tracks. **We cyclists might say that**, in that case, surely pedestrians should be made to pay as well – especially since there are far more of them than there are of us.

3 Extensive use of brackets: what are they used for?

4 Repetition for emphasis: what does this show about the writer's attitude?

5 Wanders off the subject to offer another opinion: what does this opinion reveal about the writer?

The immediate riposte to that is that charging pedestrians would not be practical – how would you collect? Which brings us back to those bells, for one idea being put forward is that, rather than carrying a permit in our wallets or a licence disc on our bikes, we should be issued with a bell to be fitted to our bikes for the double purpose of proving we've paid and satisfying the demand from other canal users for us to give better warning of our approach.

Nobody has thought through what will happen if other authorities pursue the idea – will our bikes end up bedecked with a variety of bells and horns, each with their own distinctive tone, and what sanction will be applied if you accidentally use the wrong one? Outrageous? Maybe, but it is a problem of our own making because while there are lots of complaints about inconsiderate cyclists it seems there are very few against pedestrians, except, that is, dog-walkers, who allow their animals to foul the canalpaths – and there is talk of making them take out a licence too!

The arguments had been cogent: that the human voice carries further than any bicycle bell – though not as far as an electrically powered air horn!

6 Alternates between argument and counter argument: what is his view?

7 Paints an amusing picture: what is he trying to show the reader about this idea?

8 Ends with an exclamation: what does this about what the writer thinks?

Cycling & Mountain Biking Today

As in the letter on page 77, the writer of this article uses a range of techniques to make his points effectively. One of the techniques he uses is *counter-argument*. Counter-argument occurs when a writer presents a view alternative to his own. Re-read lines 64–105. The words in bold highlight the stages of argument and counter-argument. Identify what points are made in each of these stages.

Counter-argument allows a writer to highlight the weaknesses in an alternative point of view.

Activity 7

1 Look back at the letter you wrote for Activity 5. Think about the counter-arguments that could be raised against what you said there.

2 Now list:
   • your key points
   • the points that could be made against them
   • how you could counter-argue these.

You could use a table format, like the example below.

Key point	Arguments against	How I could counter-argue
Celebrities work hard and earn their money	Working in a factory or on a building site is harder and those workers don't get paid millions.	There are many factory workers, but only one celebrity doing what he or she does.

POINTS TO REMEMBER !

❗ To argue convincingly you need to make a series of clear and logical points.

❗ Use anecdotal evidence, facts, opinions and examples to support your points.

❗ You can give your argument more impact by:
   ❐ using language emotively or humorously
   ❐ using rhetorical questions
   ❐ associating with the reader by using 'we'.

❗ Use counter-argument to show you have considered alternative points of view.

Writing your own

Now write an article for your local newspaper in which you argue, in a balanced way, that there is not enough for teenagers to do in your local area.

Follow these steps:

1 *Brainstorm ideas*
   - Think about the area. What provision is made for teenagers? Where can they go during the day?
   - Where can they go at night?

2 List five or more *key points* that you want to make and number them.

   Note what arguments could be made against them and how you could counter-argue.

   You could record your ideas in a similar chart to that used in Activity 7:

Key point	Arguments against	How I could counter-argue
1 There is nowhere to go at night apart from other people's houses.	It's safer if parents know where their child is and who they are with.	Maybe but these houses sometimes belong to older people and they're not always good places to be.

3 List *anecdotal evidence, facts, opinions and examples* you could use to support your key points. Match them, by number, to the key point they support.

   Remember these can be made up. For example, if you say over 200 teenagers between the ages of 15 and 17 live on your estate, no one will check.

4 Now decide on the order in which you are going to deal with your key points, and how you are going to organise them into paragraphs.

5 Think of a *strong opening and ending*. You could use a rhetorical question or exclamation.

6 Think about the *form of a newspaper article*. You will need a heading that catches the reader's interest and sub-headings to help organise your ideas. Writing in columns is an option when you are word-processing. You do not need to do this when you are writing by hand.

7 Now *write your article*. Re-read what you have written at the end of each paragraph. Research shows this helps to keep ideas tightly linked and coherent. It also gives you the opportunity to make changes while the ideas are still in your mind.

8 When you have finished writing your article, proofread it for errors in spelling, punctuation and grammar.

3 Writing to persuade

Persuasion in advertisements

When you are *writing to persuade*, your aim is to convince your reader. Writers of advertisements write to persuade when they try to sell products to their targeted audience. In the following example, the product is a holiday.

FELUCCAS AT DAWN, PYRAMIDS AT SUNSET, THE RED SEA AT 82°F. IT COULD ONLY BE EGYPT.

Unique on the Mediterranean's shores, a land of sun-drenched beaches and breathtaking treasures awaits your pleasure.

From Cleopatra's Alexandria to the ultra-modern
5 resorts of Sinai and the Red Sea, Egypt is an unmatchable holiday destination.

The Red Sea, for instance, boasts exhilarating water sports, pristine white beaches, lapped by crystal-clear waters, scuba-diving on tropical
10 coral reefs and five-star hotels with friendly, welcoming staff.

You'll even find lush, championship-quality golf courses to tempt your handicap if you fancy a round or two.

And just a few hours away from Egypt's holiday
15 coastlines is the unforgettable civilisation of the pharaohs, whose artifacts include some of the most spectacular finds ever unearthed.

Why not crown your Egyptian holiday with a soulful, romantic cruise along the magical Nile, stopping off to
20 explore the beautiful temple of Karnak or the magnificent Valley of the Kings?

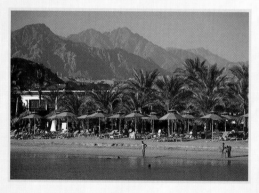

Don't forget to save a day for Cairo's colourful bazaars though. We guarantee a suitcase full of bargains,
25 if you can resist the aroma of the nearby coffee houses.

To tempt you further you'll find your travel agent has some very special deals on offer right now. For more
30 details contact the Egyptian Tourist Authority on 09001 600299 or visit www.touregypt.net

Egyptian Tourist Authority

Read the advertisement for a holiday in Egypt closely and answer the questions below.

1 Find **two** words or phrases which suggest there is no other place like Egypt.

2 The writer creates the impression that there is plenty to do in Egypt. List all the different things that the visitor could do.

3 The advertisement is packed with interesting uses of *noun phrases* (see page 74).

Compare the basic facts that 'the Red Sea has water sports, beaches with clear water, scuba-diving on coral reefs and hotels with staff,' with the description in the advertisement:

> The Red Sea, for instance, boasts exhilarating water sports, pristine white beaches lapped by crystal-clear waters, scuba diving on tropical coral reefs and five-star hotels with friendly, welcoming staff.

a List the noun phrases in a chart like the one below and explain what is suggested by each one.

b Find **five** more examples of noun phrases in the advertisement. Add them to your chart.

Noun phrases	What they suggest
exhilarating water sports	lively – invigorating – something that will make you feel good.

4 The writer has also chosen the *verbs* very carefully:

awaits (line 3) – implies it is there just for you
boasts (line 7) – suggests this is something to be proud of
lapped (line 8) – creates a sense of gentle calm

Find **four** more examples of interesting verb choices. For each one, explain what is suggested by it.

5 Read the text again and notice how the writer uses the *second person*:

> You'll even find lush, championship-quality golf courses to tempt your handicap if you fancy a round of two.

Find and note down **three** more examples of the use of the second person. What effect is the use of the second person likely to have on the reader?

Choose **two** of the following items from the box below. For each one, write a paragraph in which you aim to *persuade your reader* that it is a very desirable object. You can exaggerate, but you must not lie.

> an old, tattered teddy bear   a gold-sequinned handbag
> a set of Maths textbooks   a rusty, broken bike   a battered armchair
> a wheelbarrow with no wheel

You should aim to:
- suggest there is nothing else like it
- choose your adjectives and verbs for maximum effect
- address your reader directly in a few places.

Persuasion in appeals

Charities are not usually trying to sell a product to the reader, but the writers of charity appeals do need to write to persuade. Read the following charity appeal. What is the writer trying to persuade the reader to do?

GOMA VOLCANO CHILDREN'S APPEAL

Terror has come to the people of Goma. But this time it is not ongoing civil war or bloodshed. Lava from a violent volcanic eruption has sent half a million people fleeing
5 for their lives. At least 100,000 are small children, less than five years old.

The lava has destroyed their world. Many children have lost their homes. Some have even become separated from their parents
10 in the panic. Without shelter, food or clean water, they are all at risk from disease and malnutrition.

To help them, **UNICEF** has already sent water purification tablets, oral rehydration salts, tents,
15 tarpaulins and blankets. Four therapeutic feeding centres have also been set up to treat malnutrition.

But more life-saving supplies are urgently needed. A donation of £35, for example, could
20 buy a family kit containing essentials needed for survival. This could make the difference between life and death for these children.

They have lost everything. Please, help now.

UNICEF

In order to persuade the reader the writer of this appeal has used a number of techniques:

● Emotive use of language

This is the use of words to *appeal to the feelings* of the reader, for example:

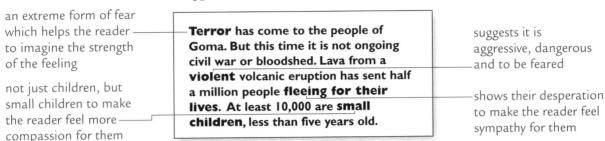

an extreme form of fear which helps the reader to imagine the strength of the feeling

not just children, but small children to make the reader feel more compassion for them

Terror has come to the people of Goma. But this time it is not ongoing civil war or bloodshed. Lava from a **violent** volcanic eruption has sent half a million people **fleeing for their lives**. At least 10,000 are **small children**, less than five years old.

suggests it is aggressive, dangerous and to be feared

shows their desperation to make the reader feel sympathy for them

● Repetition

By repeating an idea in a different way it is given *extra emphasis*, for example:

But more **life-saving** supplies are urgently needed. A donation of £35, for example, could buy a family kit containing essentials **needed for survival**. This could make **the difference between life and death** for these children.

UNICEF

In each sentence the writer reminds us that these supplies are needed to save lives. He uses different words to describe this idea in order to push the point home. He also offers an achievable target so that the readers feel they are in a position to save lives.

● Short sentences

The writer ends the appeal with two very short sentences:

They have lost everything. Please, help now.

They summarise in just a few words what the appeal is about. The word 'everything' emphasises the extent of their loss. The word 'now' emphasises the urgency of the need. Short, sharp sentences like these, when used occasionally, can be very effective.

Activity 3

Write a similar appeal for a charity of your choice. Organise your ideas into three paragraphs which describe:

- why help is needed
- what is being done already
- how the reader can help.

Aim to:

- use language emotively
- use repetition of an idea for maximum effect
- set an achievable target
- use occasional short, sharp sentences for emphasis.

Persuasion in campaigns

Charities do not only appeal to raise money. They also run campaigns to raise awareness. These campaigns are designed to persuade the reader to support a particular cause. Sometimes the writer will try to shock or disturb in order to persuade.

Study the poster below closely before answering these questions:

1 What is the link between the picture, the headline and the opening sentence?

2 What is the effect of:
   • the use of 'should' in the opening sentence
   • the repeated use of 'our' in the second sentence?

3 What is suggested by the word 'contaminated'?

4 What dangers are highlighted in the third sentence?

5 What is implied in the final sentence?

6 In what ways is the style of writing in this poster similar to or different from the advertisement and the charity appeal?

7 What is shocking or disturbing about this poster? Think about the picture and the writing.

8 This poster is designed to make the reader sit up and take notice. Do you think it is successful? Give **three** reasons for your answer.

The writing which accompanies the picture on this poster is very tightly structured in five sentences:

> **Sentence 1:** The womb should be the safest place on earth.

The writing opens with a simple statement that most people would agree with. The conditional tense 'should be' tells the reader that all is not well.

> **Sentence 2:** But today our bodies are contaminated with over 300 man-made chemicals, to which our great-grandparents were never exposed.

The conjunction 'But' placed at the start of the sentence emphasises that things are not as they should be. The word 'contaminated' has negative connotations. The use of 'our' links the writer and the reader.

> **Sentence 3:** Many of these pollutants are found in intensively-farmed food or everyday products and some have been linked with birth defects in people and wildlife.

'These pollutants' links back to the '300 man-made chemicals' of sentence 2. The sentence contains extra information and the link with 'birth defects' explains the opening sentence.

> **Sentence 4:** WWF is campaigning for the elimination of these hazardous chemicals, so that the only thing we pass on to our children is our genes.

This one-sentence paragraph explains what WWF is doing and why this action is being taken. The word 'hazardous' emphasises the danger. The second clause links back to the first sentence.

> **Sentence 5:** To find out how to help WWF and reduce your risk, call 01483 426333 or visit www.wwf.org.uk/whocares.

The use of the imperative 'call' instructs the reader to do something. This final sentence gives essential information about how to contact WWF.

Activity 5

Using one of the following starters, write the text for a campaign poster. You should write five sentences. Model your writing on the WWF text.

Schooldays should be the happiest days of our lives. But...

Britain is meant to be a nation of animal lovers. But...

Persuasion in speeches

Politicians, celebrities and other well-known people often have to make *public speeches*. In these speeches they may have to persuade the audience to a particular point of view. Sometimes these speeches are written for them.

Speeches are usually made in standard English, as they are intended to be heard by many people. A long speech needs to be tightly structured so that the audience can easily follow what is being said.

Activity 6

The six main stages of the following speech by President George Bush of the United States are outlined below. As you read the transcript of the speech, match the stages to the appropriate line numbers:

1 A description of what has happened

2 General comments on how America has responded to the attack

3 Precise details of the actions being taken

4 Offers thanks to the other countries

5 A prayer

6 Resolution for the future

lines 52–6

lines 30–45

lines 2–18

lines 57–64

lines 19–29

lines 46–51

President Bush's Address to the Nation following attacks on the World Trade Centre and the Pentagon on September 11, 2001

Good evening.

Today, our fellow citizens, our way of life, our very freedom came under attack in a series of deliberate and
5   deadly terrorist acts.

The victims were in airplanes or in their offices – secretaries, businessmen and women, military and federal workers. Moms and
10 dads. Friends and neighbors.

Thousands of lives were suddenly ended by evil, despicable acts of terror.

The pictures of airplanes flying into
15 buildings, fires burning, huge structures collapsing, have filled us with disbelief, terrible sadness and a quiet unyielding anger.

What is the impact of the repeated use of 'our'?

What is the effect of describing the victims in this way?

How is language used emotively here?

These acts of mass murder were intended to frighten our nation into chaos and
20 retreat. But they have failed. Our country is strong. A great people has been
moved to defend a great nation.

What word is repeated for emphasis?

Terrorist attacks can shake the foundations of our biggest buildings, but they
cannot touch the foundation of America. These acts shatter steel, but they
cannot dent the steel of American resolve.

What wordplay is used here? What is its effect?

25 America was targeted for attack because we're the brightest beacon for freedom
and opportunity in the world. And no one will keep that light from shining.

What image is used here? What is its effect?

How are opposites used for effect here?

Today, our nation saw evil, the very worst of human nature, and we responded
with the best of America, with the daring of our rescue workers, with the caring for
strangers and neighbors who came to give blood and help in any way they could.

30 Immediately following the first attack, I implemented our government's emergency
response plans. Our military is powerful, and it's prepared. Our emergency
teams are working in New York City and Washington DC, to help with our local
rescue efforts.

Our first priority is to get help to those who have been injured and to take
35 every precaution to protect our citizens at home and around the world from
further attacks.

How would these details help to reassure the people of America?

The functions of our government continue without interruption. Federal agencies
in Washington which had to be evacuated today are reopening for essential
personnel tonight and will be open for business tomorrow.

40 Our financial institutions remain strong, and the American economy will be
open for business as well.

Who is this message for?

The search is underway for those who are behind these evil acts. I've directed
the full resources for our intelligence and law enforcement communities to find
those responsible and bring them to justice. We will make no distinction
45 between the terrorists who committed these acts and those who harbor them.

Who is this message for?

I appreciate so very much the members of Congress who have joined me in
strongly condemning these attacks. And on behalf of the American people,
I thank the many world leaders who have called to offer their condolences
and assistance.

How does he identify himself as spokesperson for the American people?

50 America and our friends and allies join with all those who want peace and
security in the world and we stand together to win the war against terrorism.

Tonight I ask for your prayers for all those who grieve, for the children whose
worlds have been shattered, for all those whose sense of safety has been
threatened. And I pray they will be comforted by a power greater than any of
55 us spoken through the ages in Psalm 23: 'Even though I walk through the valley
of the shadow of death, I fear no evil, for You are with me.'

Why do you think he includes this psalm?

How does he appeal to feelings of patriotism?

This is a day when all
Americans from every walk
of life unite in our resolve for
60 justice and peace. America
has stood down enemies
before, and we will do so
this time.

How would you describe the tone of this final paragraph?

None of us will ever forget this
65 day, yet we go forward to
defend freedom and all that is
good and just in our world.
Thank you. Good night and
God bless America.

1 Re-read the speech and answer the questions that surround it.

2 Study the President's use of the *first-person plural* (we, our) and the *first-person singular* (I, my). Why do you think he switches between them? Write two or three sentences summarising your conclusions.

Rhetorical devices

Groups of three

In this speech President Bush frequently groups three items together. This is a commonly used *rhetorical device*: the three separate things together provide a coherent picture. Generally the most powerful idea or image is placed last for emphasis.

'Today, our fellow citizens, our way of life, our very freedom came under attack in a series of deliberate and deadly terrorist acts.' (lines 2–5)

Alliteration

President Bush occasionally uses alliteration to give particular images extra emphasis, for example:

'our biggest buildings' (line 22)

Short sentences

These are used several times throughout the speech. They allow the President to pause for dramatic effect, thus emphasising the things that are being said, for example:

'Moms and dads. Friends and neighbors.' (lines 9–10)

Look back over the speech and identify at least one other example of the use of groups of three, alliteration and short sentences.

Writing your own

You are going to write the script for either:

A speech to be given to your year group, persuading them to support the charity of your choice.

or

A speech to be given to your year group, persuading them to take an interest in the sport or cause of your choice.

To prepare this speech, which should last for between one and two minutes, follow these steps:

1 Brainstorm ideas on your chosen subject – what things can you say that will *persuade* your audience?

2 Think of how to *structure* your speech. You could adapt the structure of President Bush's speech:
   - general description of charity, sport or cause
   - general comments on it, e.g. why it needs support, how different people are involved with it
   - precise details about it and your own involvement in it
   - how your audience could help/become involved and what they would gain from this
   - final plea for support.

3 When you are writing your script, aim to:
   - include groups of three
   - identify with your audience by use of the first person plural
   - use repetition and contrast for emphasis
   - use language emotively
   - use images and wordplay for effect.

4 Keep stopping to read and improve what you have written. Imagine the words being spoken aloud. Remember your aim is to persuade your reader to become involved.

5 When you have finished your script, read it to a partner and ask for their opinion.

POINTS TO REMEMBER

! When you write to persuade your aim is to *convince your reader*.

! Persuasive writing is often packed with interesting *choices of adjectives and verbs*.

! Use the *second person* to help get and keep your reader's attention.

! *Emotive use of language and repetition* are sometimes used in persuasive writing.

! Writers may try to *shock* readers in order to persuade them.

! *Identify with your audience* by using 'we' and 'our'.

! *Groups of three, alliteration* and *short sentences* are commonly found in persuasive writing.

4 Writing to advise

Everywhere we look, in newspapers, on the net, on the walls of our schools and doctors' surgeries we find advice on how to live our lives, be better people, be thinner, be fatter, be the same, be different. But perhaps the most familiar type of writing to advise is to be found on the problem pages of magazines.

 Activity 1

Here are some common features that might be found in different types of writing to advise. Read through the **Texts A–D** and fill in the chart to identify which features appear in each of the extracts.

Writing to advise ...	Texts
Offers some further explanation	A B D
Shows some understanding of the feelings of the person seeking advice	
Is reassuring in tone	
Is challenging in tone	
Offers a solution	
Makes more than one suggestion as to what could be done	
May use non-standard English to target reader more closely	
Addresses reader directly	
Gives a warning	
Uses humour	

A **Net Natter**

I recently moved to a new school and don't have many friends yet. So I've started chatting to people on the Internet. I've become friendly
5 with one particular girl who's my age. We want to meet up, but my mum says I can't as this person may not be the person she claims to be. Doesn't this seem unfair?
10 My new mate seems really nice.

Lonely, 13, Somerset

Unfortunately, your mum has a point. Although lots of people chat on the Net for fun, there are some people who use it for other purposes. Some adults pretend to be children so they can
15 meet up with real children for illegal sexual purposes. Everyone who makes friends with someone over the Net needs to be careful. I *can* understand why you want to make new friends and your mum's concern, so why not compromise? Let her know how much meeting this person would mean to you and suggest she
20 speaks to your Net mate's mum and arranges for all of you to meet up together. That way, if this person really is a young girl, you *can* begin a new friendship safely.

Bliss

B

Getting an earful

Q **What can I do to stop my ears ringing after going to a rock concert?**

A A ringing or buzzing in the ear is known as tinnitus. And the post-gig symptom you're describing is temporary tinnitus. It's caused by
5 what's known in the trade as 'acoustic trauma' – and outside the trade as a very loud concert.

Your ears have their own complex amplification systems. Eardrums
10 transmit the sound vibrations via small bones to the delicate inner part of your ear – the cochlea – where the vibration of microscopic hairs converts it all into a message to your brain. After an
15 overdose of decibels, those hairs keep vibrating for a while, hence the tinnitus.

There's not a huge amount you can do about this except for the obvious ploys of positioning yourself well clear
20 of the speakers or developing a liking for wussy acoustic music. It's a good idea to protect your ears at other times, though – so wear some form of ear protection if you work in a noisy
25 environment, and don't crank up your Walkman too loud.

Very occasional bursts of acoustic trauma shouldn't be a great problem, but repeated or prolonged bouts can
30 lead to permanent tinnitus or deafness.

Men's Health

C

TELEPHONE TABS

My boyfriend is constantly calling me on my mobile. It makes me feel like he's checking up on me. How can I make him stop doing this?

Harassed, 15, Durham

Short of leaving your phone at home, there's no easy way to make your boyfriend back off. Trust is vital in any relationship, and he's clearly
5 lacking it! Before you act, ask yourself if you're giving him any cause for concern, and take steps to improve the situation. If it's down to his own insecurity, then you need to
10 talk. Just make sure you do so face-to-face. Keep calm, and aim to find out why he feels the need to buzz you all the time. Hopefully, with your reassurance, he'll learn that leaving
15 you alone more could bring you closer together. Ultimately you have to decide if this romance is worth sorting out in the first place. He's clearly not making you happy right
20 now, so be honest about whether that can ever change.

Bliss

NAIL BANGING

Q **Why do my toenails go black and fall off after I've played football?**

A The likely answer is that you're suffering from 'black toe nail syndrome'. This is well known to serious runners and the cause is pretty simple: as you run, your
5 toes repeatedly jam against the end of your boot. This trauma leads to bruising under the nail, which, in turn, pushes it up and away from the toe. The result? Painful black nails that, sooner or later,
10 drop off – and then grow back again.
   The cure lies in new boots: go for some between a half and one size larger that your usual size, and with plenty of width at the toes.
15 If you do lots of running between games to keep up your fitness, check that your trainers are equally roomy. And avoid downhill running as this really punishes the nails.
20 Although it can look alarming, 'black toenail syndrome' is completely harmless. It's in no way connected to rather more serious problems in which bits of your anatomy turn black and drop off – these
25 require an urgent visit to the hospital rather than the shoe shop!

Men's Health

Activity 2

Write replies to the two letters below. Each reply should be about 150 words long. Look back to Activity 1 and aim to include some, or all, of the features you had noted in the letters above.

1 For the last year my skin has been awful. I'm covered in spots and feel really embarrassed by them. Mum tells me not to worry as they'll go in a year or so but I can't wait that long. Please help.

2 My Dad's recently remarried and I visit him in his new home every week. The problem is I can't stand his wife's son. Dad expects us to be friends but he makes snide remarks behind Dad's back. Should I just ignore him?

Advice in different forms

Advice can be given in a number of different ways. Read the following two web pages before working through Activity 3.

Activity 3

Answer these questions:

1a What use is made of the question and answer approach in both web pages?

b What does this approach enable the writer to do?

c How effective do you think this is? Give two reasons for your answer.

2 What are the benefits of using a flow chart as in the first web page, when writing to advise? Give at least three benefits.

3 Why do you think the writer has used sub-headings and bullet points in the second web page?

4 Re-read the right-hand 'No' part of the flow chart.

NO

To maintain a healthy lifestyle, you should be aiming to participate in physical activity of at least moderate intensity for one hour a day. If you currently do very little activity, then you could start by aiming for half an hour a day.

Click here for ideas on how to achieve this

Write the next web page, which advises someone who does very little activity on how to start. Choose your own form for your writing.

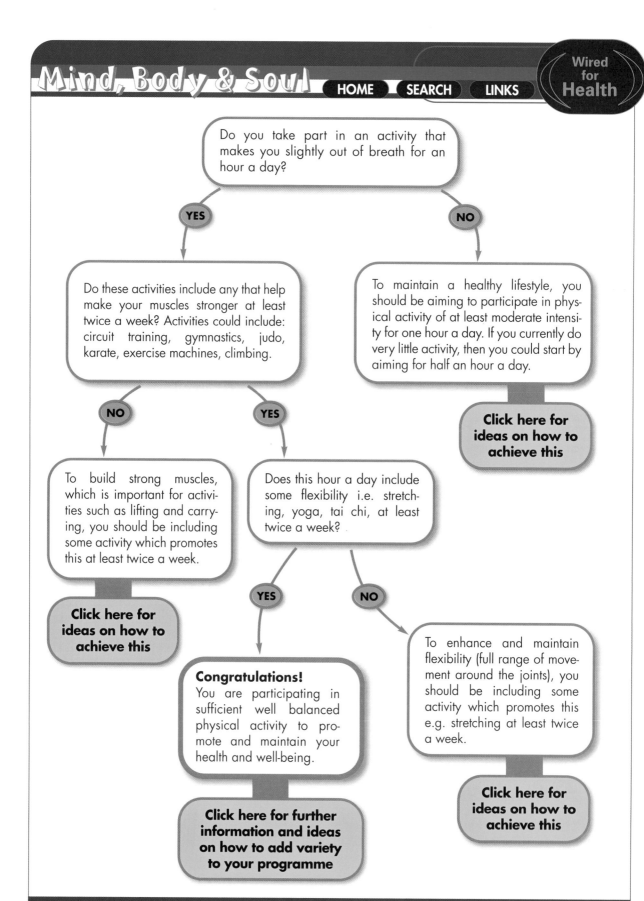

Do you take part in an activity that makes you slightly out of breath for an hour a day?

YES

NO

Do these activities include any that help make your muscles stronger at least twice a week? Activities could include: circuit training, gymnastics, judo, karate, exercise machines, climbing.

To maintain a healthy lifestyle, you should be aiming to participate in physical activity of at least moderate intensity for one hour a day. If you currently do very little activity, then you could start by aiming for half an hour a day.

NO

YES

Click here for ideas on how to achieve this

To build strong muscles, which is important for activities such as lifting and carrying, you should be including some activity which promotes this at least twice a week.

Does this hour a day include some flexibility i.e. stretching, yoga, tai chi, at least twice a week?

YES

NO

Click here for ideas on how to achieve this

Congratulations!
You are participating in sufficient well balanced physical activity to promote and maintain your health and well-being.

To enhance and maintain flexibility (full range of movement around the joints), you should be including some activity which promotes this e.g. stretching at least twice a week.

Click here for further information and ideas on how to add variety to your programme

Click here for ideas on how to achieve this

Why be active? / How much should I do? / What types of activity should I do? / One step beyond

PHYSICAL ACTIVITY ‹ ›   << BACK

What types of activity should I do?

Designing your own activity programme

When designing your activity programme, you should aim to include:

- at least one hour a day of moderate activity (activity that gets you slightly out of breath).
- at least twice a week some activity that enhances muscular strength and endurance and flexibility.

Important points to consider:

- Start off slowly and build up gradually.
- Wear clothing that allows free movement and will ensure that you feel comfortable and stay cool when participating in any physical activity.
- Don't do moderate or vigorous physical activity immediately after a heavy meal or when ill or injured.
- Always warm up before any activity and cool down afterwards.
- Vary the activities you do to avoid boredom and ensure a balance.
- If you feel any pain or discomfort, stop the activity and consult an adult.
- Chat with friends when planning your activity programme and try to do some sessions together.
- You could try encouraging members of your family to join in some of the planned sessions with you.
- Be aware of personal safety – for example, broken glass in activity areas, or traffic.

Activity Programme and Diary

Use this activity programme and diary to plan how you'll reach your activity target. Print out as many of these as you need. Remember to fill in the week number to help you keep track of what you have been doing. Use the diary

Weeks 1 and 2

Plan the activity you aim to do over the next two weeks. Use the column headed 'Activity Target' and write down the activities you plan to do and for how many minutes you plan to perform each activity.

Remember:

- You're aiming for one hour of activity per day, but it's important to start off slowly and build up gradually. Be realistic – don't expect too much too soon.
- You don't have to do the one hour of activity all at the same time. For example, you could do four different activities over a day, each lasting 15 minutes.
- If you don't do much activity at the moment, start by building up gradually.

Using different types of verbs

The type of *verb* used is a significant feature of writing to advise. You will often find extensive use of one or both of the following types:

Imperatives

These are *verbs* which can be used to:

- give orders, e.g. <u>Stop</u> smoking now!
- direct, e.g. <u>Turn</u> right at the bottom of the hill.
- make requests, e.g. <u>Open</u> the door, please.

Notice that:

- the verb is always in its basic form with no endings
- the writing is always in the present tense.

Modal verbs

There are *nine verbs* in this group:

> can, could, may, might, will, would, shall, should, must

They can only be used as *auxiliary verbs*, which means they must be linked together with another verb.

They are used to express such ideas as:

- possibility, e.g. You <u>might</u> be able to go there.
- willingness, e.g. Together, we <u>can</u> do this.
- necessity, e.g. They <u>must</u> arrive on time.

Note that the verbs *dare*, *need*, *ought to*, *have to* and *used to* have a very similar function and act like modals.

Activity 4

1 Identify and list examples of the use of *imperatives*, *modal verbs* and verbs which act as modals in the **Texts** (**A–D**) and the web pages.

2 Write a page for your school web site in which you advise incoming Year 7 pupils how to make the most of their first year. Think about how you could best present your advice on a web page.

 Aim to include:

 - questions and answers
 - bullet points
 - imperatives
 - modal verbs.

Features of writing to advise

Read the extract below, taken from a traveller's handbook, and work through Activity 5.

Activity 5

1 As you read, record by line number and phrases, evidence of:
   - interesting use of language
   - a wide vocabulary range
   - humour.

You could record your evidence on a simple chart like this:

Interesting use of language	Wide vocabulary range	Humour
(line 8) sleek speed	(line 7) curiously engaging	

2 What is the effect of these on the reader?

The name of the game

Everyone has an animal they really really want to see more than any other. Elephants, lion, buffalo, leopards and rhinos are the classic 'Big Five' species. For some people, the gawky
5 giraffe with its supermodel legs and eyelashes-to-die-for is top of the list, others find grunting warthogs curiously engaging, plenty want to witness the sleek speed of the cheetah.

It's best not to get too obsessed about
10 ticking off a list, however. No matter what the brochures tell you, there are no guarantees that you will see everything on one trip. Animals have their own patterns and, while experienced guides can second-guess where
15 they might be at any given time, this isn't fool-proof. And animals are no fools. In some reserves, cheetahs have wised up to fact that most game drives take place in the early morning or late afternoon and have started to
20 avoid going out at those times. For that reason, it's best to spend a few days in one reserve. Relax, soak up the glory of the bush and of the more common creatures. The Big Five will probably stroll up – eventually. If you
25 only have a week, try to spend it at one place or, at most, split it between two. You can cram

in more reserves if you try hard, but will probably see less. And you will be very sore from bumpy travel.

Safari etiquette

30 Game reserves seem so vast that it's easy to forget they are home for numerous animals, which were there first but may not be for much longer if their habitat and habits are not protected. The rules of the wild are essential
35 for your enjoyment, your safety and their survival:

▪ Most parks have a list of rules that they give out as you enter. Stick to them. Most close at sundown – make sure you're out by then or in

40 a game lodge or camp. If you miss this and can't leave for any reason as night falls, stay in your car until found – all night, if necessary.

▨ Make sure that you/your driver stick to designated tracks. Off-road driving injures
45 smaller game, particularly young animals concealed in bushes and grass.

▨ Don't under any circumstances follow a predator chasing dinner. The chances of a successful kill are greatly hampered if a lioness
50 or cheetah is accompanied by a crashing jeep.

▨ Don't join the vultures circling the feast. It's better to watch animals with their kill from a distance. Some animals are so used to the presence of cars that they will carry
55 on eating, if you don't get too close. Others will abandon their meal altogether and then have to summon up the massive energy needed to make another kill – they don't get take-aways.
60 ▨ Stick to the speed limit. Your chances of spotting animals are greatly increased, and slowness gives you time to stop should an animal leap out onto the road.
65 ▨ Blend into the surroundings (as much as you can in a lumbering Land Rover). Leave bright coloured clothes at home. Be very silent in the presence of animals. Loud cries of 'cute, amazing,

70 wonderful, awesome, did you ever, oh my' are just not on. They frighten the animals and ruin the spectacle. Persistent offenders are at risk from their fellow travellers, who may want to throttle them with the nearest camera strap.

75 ▨ Don't interact with the animals in any way. This means not feeding them – people have lost fingers giving bananas to baboons. It also means not provoking them by revving the engine, making sudden movements or
80 calling out to them. No big cat is going to obey calls of 'here kitty kitty' (this has been heard – honestly).

'**The safari traveller**' by Amy Sohanpaul from *The Traveller's Handbook*

As well as using a wide vocabulary and a range of interesting images, this writer also creates interest by using a variety of sentence structures:

● **Simple sentences,** which communicate one idea, e.g.: 'Stick to the speed limit.' (line 60) The writer uses the imperative to stress the importance of her advice.

● **Compound sentences,** which link two or more simple sentences with a conjunction such as *and, but,* and *or,* e.g.: 'They frighten the animals and ruin the spectacle.' (lines 71–2) The writer links two different and convincing reasons to follow her advice.

● **Complex sentences,** which communicate more than one idea by using two or more clauses, sometimes separated by commas, e.g.: 'Game reserves seem so vast that it's easy to forget they are home for numerous animals, which were there first but may not be for much longer if their habitat and habits are not protected.' (lines 30–4) The writer uses complex sentences to follow through the cause and effect in her advice.

- **Conditional sentences,** which are a form of complex sentence. They show how, if one course of action is taken, then another is likely to follow. Conditional sentences often contain the conjunction *if*, e.g.: 'Some animals are so used to the presence of cars that they will carry on eating, if you don't get too close.' (lines 53–5) The writer provides motivation for following her advice.

Writing your own

Now write a single-page advice leaflet on:

How to survive GCSEs.

Your readers are students just starting Year 10.

Follow these steps:

1 *Brainstorm ideas* for what to put in your advice leaflet. It might help you to think about:

> subjects   teachers   workload   parents
> social life   stress   coursework

2 Think about *how to present your ideas*. Aim for some variety in your presentation. You could include a question and answer section, bullet points, a flow diagram and a prose section with a range of continuous sentences.

3 Decide on the *order* for your ideas. Think about how to attract and keep your readers' attention. What point do you want to end on and leave in the reader's mind?

4 Read back through this unit to remind yourself of the various *features of writing to advise*. Aim to include as many of these as you can in your writing.

5 *Address your reader directly* and, above all, aim to make your writing interesting by using:
   - a range of images and vocabulary
   - a variety of sentence structures.

POINTS TO REMEMBER

! *Writing to advise* is sometimes reassuring and sometimes challenging.

! Writing to advise can take a number of *different forms*.

! *Imperative and modal verbs* are often used in writing to advise.

! Aim to use a *range of vocabulary and sentence structures*, including *conditional sentences*.

Now that you have developed the skills you need for Paper 1 Section B, you can start to look at the types of questions you might come across in your examination. In this section of the exam you are given a choice of writing tasks from which you should choose one. The types of writing tested here are writing which argues, persuades or advises. In the exam they may be combined.

The exam questions on the following pages are linked to the same topics or themes as the non-fiction and media texts used in the Section A Exam Practice papers (pages 54–65). Remind yourself of the materials used in Section A before you start work on Section B, but do not be tempted to copy from them.

Your teacher will tell you whether you should work on Foundation or Higher Tier.

Making your choice and planning your ideas

Make sure you take time to think about which task to do. It is important that you:

• choose the task which gives you the opportunity to write well

• have plenty of ideas to write about.

Read all the options carefully and consider what you could write for each one.

Once you have made your choice, you are ready to start planning. In the exam you should spend about five minutes planning and sequencing your material. For these practice questions it will probably take you longer than that.

Remember that the plan is for *your* benefit. It will help you produce a well-structured and interesting piece of writing. You will not be directly assessed on your plan in the exam but without it you are less likely to produce a good piece of writing. **The examiner comments** section on pages 109–10 takes you through the stages you need to work through before starting to write your answer.

Paper 1 Section B: Writing

Answer **one** question in this Section.

Spend about **45 minutes** on this Section.

You may use some of the information from Section A (pages 54–65) if you want to, but you do not have to do so. If you use any of the information do not simply copy it.

Remember to:
- Spend about 5 minutes planning and sequencing your material
- Write about 1½ sides in your answer book
- Spend about 5 minutes checking
  - ✓ your paragraphing   ✓ your punctuation   ✓ your spelling.

Either

1 Write an article for a magazine in which you **argue** that more money should be given to the poorer peoples of the world. You should aim to:
- make your key points clearly
- support your argument with evidence and examples.

Or

2 Write a letter to a celebrity of your choice. Your aim is to **persuade** him or her to support a particular charity. You should aim to:
- give reasons why he or she should support the charity
- use language to persuade.

Or

3 Write the advice sheet that **either** Children in Need **or** Red Nose Day could send out to secondary schools. Its aim is to **advise** students on how to raise money. You should aim to:
- make suggestions about the kinds of things students could do
- advise students of the difficulties or dangers of some fund-raising activities.

4 Your tutor group has decided to raise money for Plan International (see pages 56–7). Write the script for a speech to be given to other students in your year, in which you:
- **argue** that Plan International is a good choice
- use language that will **persuade** them to support it.

Exam Practice Higher Tier

Paper 1 Section B: Writing

Answer **one** question in this Section.

Spend about **45 minutes** on this Section.

You may use some of the information from Section A (pages 54–65) if you want to, but you do not have to do so. If you use any of the information do not simply copy it.

> Remember to:
> - Spend about 5 minutes planning and sequencing your material
> - Write about 1½ sides in your answer book
> - Spend about 5 minutes checking
>   ✓ your paragraphing ✓ your punctuation ✓ your spelling.

Either

1 Write an article for a magazine in which you **argue** that more money should be given to the poorer peoples of the world.

Or

2 Write a letter to a celebrity of your choice in which you try to **persuade** him or her to support a particular charity.

Or

3 Write the advice sheet that **either** Children in Need **or** Red Nose Day could send out to secondary schools. Its aim is to **advise** students on what they should and shouldn't do in order to raise money.

Or

4 Your tutor group has decided to raise money for Plan International (see pages 62–3). Write the script for a speech to be given to other students in your year, in which you:
   - **argue** that Plan International is a good choice
   - use language that will **persude** them to support it.

The examiner comments ...

You will have noticed that the questions for both tiers are basically the same, although for the Foundation Tier questions, you are sometimes given suggestions to help you. The questions in the exam will not always be identical but are often very similar. Questions on the type of writing – writing to argue, persuade or advise – may be combined.

Before writing your answer to your chosen question, follow these steps. The first task on the Foundation Tier is used as an example here:

> Write an article for a magazine in which you **argue** that more money should be given to the poorer peoples of the world.
>
> You should aim to:
> - make your key points clearly
> - support your argument with evidence and examples.

Step 1: Identify your purpose, audience and form

Purpose: to argue that more money should be given to the poorer peoples of the world.
Audience: readers of a magazine; your examiner.
Form: an article for a magazine.

Step 2: Gather ideas

Brainstorm ideas relevant to the task:

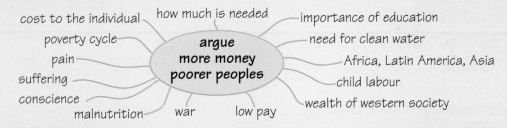

Step 3: Start to link your ideas

You could do this by numbering or colour-coding points in your diagram or by listing them as below:
Conditions: pain, suffering, malnutrition, disease, lack of clean water
Education: many illiterate, can't break out of poverty cycle, child labour
Why we should help: wealth in West, things we regard as necessities, conscience

Step 4: Sequence your ideas

Now you have several groups of ideas that will form the basis of your writing. You need to sequence these into the order in which you will write about them. These groups could form the basis of your paragraphs:

a Describe what conditions are like in parts of the world.

b Point to the wealth of the West as a reason to help.

c Show how education could be used to help break the poverty cycle.

d Argue that we have a moral obligation to help – to sit back and ignore this is to allow people to die ...

Step 5: Think about the type of writing

Use the *Points to remember* boxes at the end of each unit to help you focus on the features of the type of writing you have selected:

- To argue convincingly you need to make a series of clear and logical points.
- Use anecdotal evidence, facts, opinions and examples to support your points.
- You can give your argument more impact by:
  - ❏ using language emotively or humorously
  - ❏ using rhetorical questions
  - ❏ associating with the reader by using 'we'
  - ❏ using a range of sentence structures.
- Use counter-argument to show you have considered alternative points of view.

Where appropriate, use these points to develop your plan.

Step 6: Think about form

Lastly, think about the form your writing is to take and the features of this form. Is it a letter, leaflet, article or advice sheet? You may want to produce a headline and some sub-headings for your magazine article. But, as this is handwritten and not word-processed, you should not attempt to write in columns.

Once you have worked through Steps 1–6 you are ready to start writing.

Check and revise your writing

Always keep five minutes at the end of the exam to check and correct your work. This should not be confused with redrafting your work, which is the process of reorganising, improving and rewriting which you will be familiar with in coursework.

In those five minutes you should aim to:

- Re-read what you have written. Allow each word on the page to register in your head as though you were reading it aloud. Alter sentences that do not make sense.
- Correct errors in punctuation and spelling. Watch out particularly for things where you know you tend to make mistakes.
- Improve what you've written, by adding or deleting certain words, or changing the punctuation, but take care to make sure each sentence still makes sense.
- Make sure your ending has impact. If not, develop it.

Paper 2

This paper examines **Reading** in Section A and **Writing** in Section B. Each section is worth 15% of your final mark for English.

Paper 2 (1 hour 30 minutes)

Section A requires reading responses to poetry drawn from different cultures and traditions in Part 1 of the **AQA A Anthology**.

Section B requires one piece of writing which informs, explains or describes; some of the tasks may be linked thematically to the poems in the **Anthology**.

Section A: *Reading Poems from Different Cultures and Traditions*

You will study the poems in the **Anthology** in school.

In your exam you will be asked to answer **one question** from a choice of two. In each question there will be **one named poem**.

The Assessment Objectives for Paper 2 Section A are to:

- read with insight and engagement
- make appropriate references to texts
- develop and sustain interpretations of texts
- select material appropriate to purpose
- collate material from different sources and make cross references
- understand and evaluate linguistic devices
- understand and evaluate structural and presentational devices
- comment on ways language varies and changes.

In the **Anthology** there are sixteen poems grouped into two clusters. In this section you will focus on **two** of these poems – one from each cluster – and explore them with a focus on the Assessment Objectives. The skills you develop in your work on these two poems will help you as you study other poems in the section of the **Anthology** for the English examination.

1 Exploring poems from different cultures

This section explores texts that come originally from cultures that are not English. The poems in the two clusters reflect *different cultures and traditions* in a variety of ways. They may be:

- about aspects of life in different countries
- about familiar topics and themes which are explored in a different setting from an English one
- written in ways that are different from mainstream English poetry.

Although they are written in English and may have been written in England, the writers have usually been born or lived abroad. You will find some unusual words and names of people or places that you might have to research.

The word *culture* is used here to describe the range of ideas, beliefs, values and knowledge that are inherited by particular groups of people. It is something that is shared by one group of people and marks them out as different from other groups. Within one broad culture it is possible to have many different cultures.

While 'culture' has a broader meaning, the term *traditions* refers more specifically to the customs handed down from one generation to another. Within a culture, you would find particular traditions that help to define that culture.

Activity 1

1 Discuss the list below with a partner and decide if they are things which are *important* in defining English culture. What other things might you add to the list?
   - the English language
   - Shakespeare
   - English history
   - Christianity
   - tea.

2 Make another list of any *traditions* which you feel are very 'English'. For example, you may feel that letting off fireworks on 5 November is an English tradition.

3 Choose another country that you have some knowledge of. You, or someone in your group, might have been born or have roots in another country; you might know about a country like America from TV programmes and films. Make notes on how the culture and traditions of this other country are different from England's.

Read the following account of a traditional Hindu wedding. Make notes on the similarities and differences with a traditional English wedding.

Similarities	Differences

The wedding ceremony usually lasts about an hour, but the celebrations often go on for several days. The wedding takes place either in a temple or the bride's home. The bride wears special eye make-up, and a dye is used to make patterns on her hands and feet. She wears a new red and gold sari, and lots of gold jewellery. Preparing the bride for the
5 ceremony takes several hours. Both the bride and groom wear garlands of flowers.

The first part of the wedding is when the bride's father welcomes the bridegroom. The bridegroom sits under a special canopy, which is a
10 decorated covering. He is given small presents which are symbols of happiness and a good life. Then the bride arrives, usually wearing a veil so that her face cannot be seen. She
15 removes this during the ceremony. The couple sit in front of a special fire. Their right hands are tied together and holy water is sprinkled on them when the bride's father
20 'gives' her to the bridegroom. There are prayers and offerings of rice.

The most important part of the ceremony is when the bride and groom take seven steps towards the
25 fire. At each step they stop and make promises to each other. While they do this, they are joined by a piece of cloth. It is hung loosely round the bridegroom's neck, and tied to the
30 bride's sari. This is a symbol that they are being joined as husband and wife. Once they have taken the steps together, they are married. There are more prayers and readings, and
35 flower petals are thrown before the guests give their wedding presents. Then everyone shares a meal.

Read **Texts A–D** below, taken from some of the poems in the **Anthology** and decide what is 'different' about the culture from which the poem comes. Write your findings in the chart in note form.

Think about:

- the *language* used
- *ideas* which seem 'different'
- *behaviour* which seems different.

A

> They picked Akanni up one morning
> Beat him soft like clay
> And stuffed him down the belly
> Of a waiting jeep.
> What business of mine is it
> So long they don't take the yam
> From my savouring mouth?

from **Not My Business** by Niyi Osundare

B

> ...if
> a toktaboot
> thi trooth
> lik wanna yoo
> scruff...

from **Unrelated Incidents** by Tom Leonard

D

> The peasants came like swarms of flies
> and buzzed the name of God a hundred times
> to paralyse the Evil One.
> With candles and with lanterns
> throwing giant scorpion shadows
> on the mud-baked walls
> they searched for him: ...

from **Night of the Scorpion** by Nissim Ezekiel

C

> Sometimes I saw Lahore –
> my aunts in shaded rooms,
> screened from male visitors...

from **Presents from my Aunts in Pakistan** by Moniza Alvi

Text	Language used	Different ideas	Different behaviour
A			

POINT TO REMEMBER !

! It is important that you are able to comment on how the poems reflect *different* cultures and traditions.

2 Reading with insight and engagement

Reading with *insight* and *engagement* is about getting to grips with a text and considering its meaning. Poetry is a very individual and expressive writing form.

- It is often presented differently on a page to other kinds of text.
- Language is often used in unusual, thought-provoking ways.
- The ideas being explored may be new and difficult to follow.

Very few people fully understand a poem the first time they read it. That is why it is important to *engage* with the poem, to re-read it several times and spend some time trying to get under its skin. As you study a poem you begin to uncover different layers of meaning. It is important to be aware of the range of possible *meanings*: often there are many different ways to read a text.

Activity 1

1 The poem you are going to explore has an unusual title: **Two Scavengers in a Truck, Two Beautiful People in a Mercedes.** Before you read the poem, brainstorm some ideas and questions you have in response to the title. Put the title in the centre of a page and surround it with your notes and questions.

2 It is always helpful to begin by getting some 'basics' clear. Start by answering these questions:
   a Where and when is the setting for the poem?
   b Where are the two 'beautiful people' going?
   c Where are the 'two scavengers' going?
   d What happens?

Two Scavengers in a Truck, Two Beautiful People in a Mercedes

At the stoplight waiting for the light
               nine a.m. downtown San Francisco
a bright yellow garbage truck
        with two garbagemen in red plastic blazers
5   standing on the back stoop
            one on each side hanging on
and looking down into
            an elegant open Mercedes
      with an elegant couple in it
10 The man
        in a hip three-piece linen suit
           with shoulder-length blond hair & sunglasses
The young blond woman so casually coifed
          with a short skirt and colored stockings
15   on the way to his architect's office

And the two scavengers up since four a.m.
                          grungy from their route
                on the way home
        The older of the two with grey iron hair
                              and hunched back
            looking down like some
                          gargoyle Quasimodo
        And the younger of the two
                    also with sunglasses & long hair
            about the same age as the Mercedes driver

        And both scavengers gazing down
                              as from a great distance
                at the cool couple
            as if they were watching some odorless TV ad
                    in which everything is always possible

        And the very red light for an instant
                    holding all four close together
            as if anything at all were possible
                              between them
            across that small gulf
                    in the high seas
                              of this democracy

Lawrence Ferlinghetti

1 The poem's title shows that it is going to concern two pairs of people from different social classes – rich and poor. The first 25 lines are a description of these two pairs and the place they meet. Copy and complete the chart below with the words and phrases used to describe each of the four characters.

Character	Words and phrases used
The beautiful young man	'In a hip three-piece suit'
The young blond woman	
The older scavenger	
The younger scavenger	

2 How can you tell what the poet *feels* about these characters and the differences between them? In your answer, refer to some of the words and phrases from the list you compiled in question 1.

3 In the final twelve lines of the poem, the poet reflects on the scene he has just described. What is the 'small gulf' he writes about?

4 The poet uses the words 'as if' and 'possible' twice during the course of the poem.

> as if they were watching some odorless TV ad
>   in which everything is always possible
>
> as if anything at all were possible
>   between them

   a What is it that might seem 'possible'?
   b What does the phrase 'as if' suggest about the poet's feelings about these possibilities?

5 The poem captures a particular moment in America in which two very different kinds of people are 'frozen in time'. The poet clearly feels there is something of importance in this brief and uneventful moment. What point do you think he was trying to make?

POINT TO REMEMBER !

! You need to work out what the poet thinks and what message s/he is trying to get across to the reader.

3 Developing and sustaining an interpretation

Your *interpretation* of a poem is your idea of what the poem is about. To *develop and sustain* your idea, you need to take your interpretation further and work through the different parts of the poem which provide the evidence for your idea.

Here are three possible interpretations of Ferlinghetti's poem:

A

He doesn't take sides: he shows America as a 'democracy' in which everyone has chances. He's showing that the two garbagemen have the chance to be rich like the elegant couple.

B

He's on the side of the two garbagemen. His purpose is to show his dislike for rich people and a society that is unfair.

C

He thinks that the idea of 'democracy' – that everyone has equal opportunities – is a sham, and this poem shows it. There is a huge gap between rich and poor and little chance of it being bridged.

Activity 1

1 Study the interpretations above. Find and list evidence to support each interpretation.

Interpretation	Evidence from poem

2 Now weigh up the evidence and decide which view you most agree with. Think about:

- how each of the two groups is described and explore whether the poet's feelings about the characters can be discovered
- how the writer draws attention to the *similarities* and *differences* between the two groups.
- what the writer says in the final twelve lines of the poem where he moves from describing the scene to commenting on it.

Making appropriate references to the text

It is very important to *explain* your ideas about the poem. To do this you need to refer to those parts of the poem that provide evidence to support your ideas. 'Appropriate' references are those that are:

- *relevant* to the idea you are developing
- of a *suitable length* so that the flow of your writing is not interrupted.

1 You can make appropriate references in different ways:

   a You refer to the text *in your own words*, e.g.:

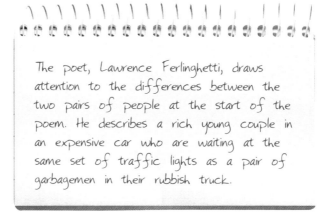

The poet, Lawrence Ferlinghetti, draws attention to the differences between the two pairs of people at the start of the poem. He describes a rich young couple in an expensive car who are waiting at the same set of traffic lights as a pair of garbagemen in their rubbish truck.

   b Sometimes you may want to *quote directly from the text*.

   - You can include significant words and phrases in the flow of your writing, e.g.:

Ferlinghetti repeats the word 'elegant' in his description of the rich couple and you wonder if he is being sincere or if there is a note of sarcasm.

and

The writer describes the oldest garbageman as though he has had a tough life: 'with grey iron hair/and hunched back'.

Notice how / is used to show a line break.

   - When you need to use slightly longer quotations, these should be set out on new lines within your paragraph, e.g.:

There is never any indication in the poem that the rich pair are at all aware of the two garbagemen. It is the garbagemen who notice the rich pair:

'looking down into
        an elegant open Mercedes'.

2 Strike a balance when using quotations. You need to provide evidence from the text to support your main points, but using too many quotations will interrupt the flow of your writing and the development of your ideas.

3 There is a useful formula you can apply when *writing a response to a text*. It shows the connection between 'reading with insight', 'making appropriate references to the text', and 'developing and sustaining interpretations':

- introduce an idea (*insight*)
- refer appropriately to the text to indicate where the idea is based (*appropriate reference*)
- develop the idea further (*sustaining an interpretation*).

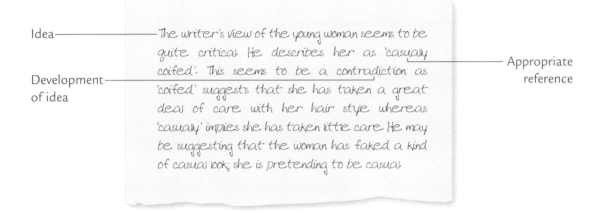

Idea ———— The writer's view of the young woman seems to be quite critical. He describes her as 'casually coifed'. This seems to be a contradiction as 'coifed' suggests that she has taken a great deal of care with her hair style whereas 'casually' implies she has taken little care. He may be suggesting that the woman has faked a kind of casual look; she is pretending to be casual.

Development of idea

Appropriate reference

Activity **2**

Write about the writer's presentation of the two scavengers in the poem. Use appropriate references to the poem.

POINTS TO REMEMBER **!**

! Poems have different layers of meaning. You need to study the poems closely to be aware of these.

! Always support the points you make by referring to the poem. Aim to strike a balance between using your own words and using quotations.

Looking at linguistic devices

When you are writing about a poet's use of linguistic devices you are exploring the use of language. When writing about poetry, never just 'spot' things like similes and list them. 'Understand and evaluate' means you need to be able to *explain* the poet's *use* of these devices and their effect on the reader.

Activity 1

Re-read the poem **Two Scavengers in a Truck** on pages 116–17.

1 Look at the effect of *single words* in the poem.
   - What is the effect of using the word 'scavengers' to describe the two garbagemen?
   - What is the effect of the word 'cool', used to describe the couple in the Mercedes?

2 *Juxtaposition* is a term that describes the placing of things together. What are the effects of the following phrases in which words are surprisingly placed next to each other?
   - 'casually coifed'   • 'small gulf'

3 Look at the imagery of the poem: metaphor and simile. Complete the following chart to comment on the effects of some of the *metaphors* and *similes*. One example has been done for you.

Imagery	What are the effects of the imagery?
'hunched back/looking down like some/gargoyle Quasimodo'	
The two garbagemen look at the young couple 'as if they were watching some odorless TV ad/in which everything is always possible'	
'stoplight' or 'red light'	This is a metaphor for a brief period of time. The rich and poor couples have been brought together for only a few brief moments simply because a red traffic light has stopped both vehicles. Everyone knows that in a few seconds the light will change to green and rich and poor will go their separate ways – it's only accidental that they seem close to each other.
'the high seas/of this democracy'	

Looking at structural and presentational devices

Poets shape their poems very carefully. Words, lines and stanzas are arranged for effect: lines may be grouped into clusters; a single word may be displayed on a line of its own.

Activity (2)

1 Look at the poem on pages 116–17 again. It is possible to break it down into five sections. Work out what idea or subject is explored by the poet in each of the following sections:

Lines	Idea or subject
1–9	
10–15	
16–25	
26–30	
31–37	

2 Here are the five opening lines of the poem without any line breaks:

> 'At the stoplight waiting for the light nine a.m. downtown San Francisco a bright yellow garbage truck with two garbagemen in red plastic blazers standing on the back stoop'

a Explain in a short paragraph why you think the poet put line breaks where they are in the final version of the poem.

b Choose a section of the poem from the chart in question 1 and write an explanation of why those lines are broken up as they are.

POINTS TO REMEMBER !

! Never just 'spot and list' things like similes and metaphors. Comment on what effect the writer achieves by using them.

! Writers think carefully about how to arrange words in lines and on the page. Be prepared to write about this and to give reasons for why a particular form has been chosen.

5 Developing your skills

You have explored:

- reading with insight and engagement
- developing and sustaining an interpretation
- understanding linguistic, structural and presentational devices.

You are now going to develop these skills as you explore the poem **Half-Caste**.

Reading with insight and engagement

Read the poem **Half-Caste** by John Agard several times before working through Activity 1 below.

Activity 1

1 In the first three lines the speaker uses the term 'half-caste'. The rest of the poem is a response to the use of that term. In lines 4–30 the speaker uses three different examples to explain why the term 'half-caste' should not be used.

List the *three examples* and explain how they are used to criticise use of the term 'half-caste'.

2 Having used these examples, how does the writer change the way he writes about the use of 'half-caste' in lines 31–46?

3 At the end of the poem the speaker tells the listener to:

> . . . come back tomorrow
> wid de whole of yu eye
> and de whole of yu ear
> an de whole of yu mind

What is being suggested here about people who use the term 'half-caste'?

4 Working with a partner, discuss which words could be used to describe the mood of the poem. For each word you use, provide a brief explanation and quotation to support your idea.

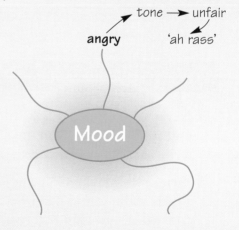

Half-Caste

Excuse me
standing on one leg
I'm half-caste

Explain yuself
5 wha yu mean
when yu say half-caste
yu mean when picasso
mix red an green
is a half-caste canvas/
10 explain yuself
wha yu mean
when yu say half-caste
yu mean when light an shadow
mix in de sky
15 is a half-caste weather/
well in dat case
england weather
nearly always half-caste
in fact some o dem cloud
20 half-caste till dem overcast
so spiteful dem don't want de sun pass
ah rass/
explain yuself
wha yu mean
25 when yu say half-caste
yu mean tchaikovsky
sit down at dah piano
an mix a black key
wid a white key
30 is a half-caste symphony/

Explain yuself
wha yu mean
Ah listening to yu wid de keen
half of mih ear
35 Ah lookin at yu wid de keen
half of mih eye
and when I'm introduced to yu

I'm sure you'll understand
why I offer yu half-a-hand
40 an when I sleep at night
I close half-a-eye
consequently when I dream
I dream half-a-dream
an when moon begin to glow
45 I half-caste human being
cast half-a-shadow
but yu must come back tomorrow
wid de whole of yu eye
an de whole of yu ear
50 an de whole of yu mind

an I will tell yu
de other half
of my story.

John Agard

Developing and sustaining interpretations

Half-Caste and **Two Scavengers** are quite long poems. To explore how the poets develop their ideas, you need to respond to the different stages of the poems.

Activity 2

Write an explanation of how the poet's ideas about the use of the term 'half-caste' are developed in the course of the poem. You should:

- explore how the poet uses examples up to line 30
- explore how the poet takes a more personal approach from line 31
- give your response to the term 'half-caste' and the poet's.

Looking at aspects of structure: rhyme and repetition

Two Scavengers in a Truck is not a rhyming poem, whereas there is quite a lot of rhyme and repetition in **Half-Caste**.

One way poets draw attention to particular words, phrases and ideas is by repeating them. Rhyme can also be used to draw attention to key words.

Activity 3

1 Find the places in **Half-Caste** where the words 'Explain yuself/wha yu mean/when yu say half-caste?' are repeated. What are the effects of repeating them so often?

2 In lines 48–50 the poet repeats the phrase 'de whole of yu...' three times. He could have simply written 'wid de whole of yu eye, ear and mind'. What effect does the *repetition* of the phrase have on the reader?

3 The poet uses *rhyme*. Look at this section about Tchaikovsky.

> yu mean tchaikovsky
> sit down at dah piano
> an mix a black key
> wid a white key
> is a half-caste symphony/

The rhyming brings all three words together logically – they are all words associated with *music*.

Now look at lines 38–9 and 42–7. How do these rhymes contrast with the rhymes in lines 26–30? Explain how the poet's use of these sound effects might influence the reader.

POINT TO REMEMBER

! Read the poems aloud and listen to them being read aloud. This will help you to notice the impact of rhymes and repetition.

6 Looking at two poems

Exploring how language varies and changes

To meet this Assessment Objective you need to be aware of how writers use language in different ways, sometimes depending on what part of the world they come from.

Activity 1

1 **Two Scavengers in a Truck, Two Beautiful People in a Mercedes** (pages 116–17) is written by an American poet, who uses vocabulary such as 'downtown', which you might not expect to find in a poem by an English writer. List the other examples of American vocabulary in the poem.

2 The poet uses some American slang: 'hip', 'cool' and 'grungy'. The first two words are used to describe the 'elegant' young people and the second describes the two garbagemen.

   a Look at the poem again to see where each slang word is used. Discuss the meaning of each word and make short lists of other words that are close in meaning.

   b Discuss what the three slang words – 'hip', 'cool' and 'grungy' – tell us about the poet's view of these people.

Activity 2

One of the most obvious features of **Half-Caste** is the way the language varies from standard English. John Agard has a West Indian background and is well known for his poetry readings.

1 Re-read the opening three lines of the poem. They *are* written in standard English. Why?

2 The spelling of many words varies from standard English; the grammar is also different. How does the following section of the poem differ from conventional grammar?

> 'yu mean tchaikovsky
> sit down at dah piano
> an mix a black key
> wid a white key
> is a half-caste symphony/'

3 This is a poem *about* use of language – about the use of a word like 'half-caste'. Give reasons explaining why you think the poet chose to express his ideas using a West Indian dialect.

4 Identify parts of the poem *after* the first three lines which are written in standard English. Why do you think the poet has used some standard English in a poem which is mainly written in dialect?

Selecting material appropriate to purpose

In the exam you will usually be asked to write about **two** poems. There will be *key words* in the question which show what you should focus on in the poems.

You will need to select relevant material from the poems in order to support your response to the key points in the question. For example, if you were asked to explore the ways people are presented in **Two Scavengers in a Truck** (pages 116–17), there are certain lines which would be particularly important.

(pages 116–17)

Activity 3

1 Highlight the key words in the question:

Explore the ways in which people are presented in *Two Scavengers in a Truck.*

2 Identify parts of the poem which describe each of the two scavengers.

3 Which lines would you focus on to show how the writer presents the two 'beautiful people'?

Collating material from different sources

When looking at two poems you will need to include relevant textual references from both of the poems. This process, known as collation, involves *examining* and *comparing* the different texts.

Now you are going to compare the ways people are presented in **Two Scavengers** and **Half-Caste**. Remember that in **Half-Caste** 'people' could refer to the speaker and whoever he is addressing. You will need to think about how the two poets present people in *similar and/or different ways*.

Activity 4

Write down your ideas about the *similarities* and *differences* between the poems. Think about:

- what you find out about the people, for example their appearance, the way they talk, their feelings
- the methods the poets use to present these people
- what you learn about the poets' attitudes to these people.

Cross referencing

In Activity 4 you have made cross references by linking different points in two poems. When you are writing about one part of a poem, and you draw attention to another part of the same poem, you are also *cross referencing*.

Activity 5

1 John Agard uses the example of 'picasso' to explore the stupidity of referring to a human being as 'half' something. Later in the poem he refers to 'tchaikovsky' – another example drawn from the world of the arts. Explain the effect of referring to two artists to make his point.

2 In **Two Scavengers in a Truck**, where might you make a cross reference to the following:
   - the mention of the 'stoplight' in the opening line?
   - the hair and sunglasses of the 'beautiful' young man?
   - the idea of 'looking down' that appears in line 7 of the poem?

   For each one, explain the significance of the cross reference.

POINTS TO REMEMBER

! If the poet has used non-standard English, you need to consider the reasons for this and to explain the effects achieved through it.

! Key words will help you to select appropriate material.

! Make sure you make cross references within one poem *and* between two poems.

7 Writing about two poems

In the exam you will have about 40 minutes to produce a piece of writing about two poems from the *Different Cultures* section of the **Anthology**. It is important to answer the question. Never be tempted to write down *all* you know about the two poems.

How to structure a response

There are two main ways you can structure your response. These share many common features, as shown in this flow diagram:

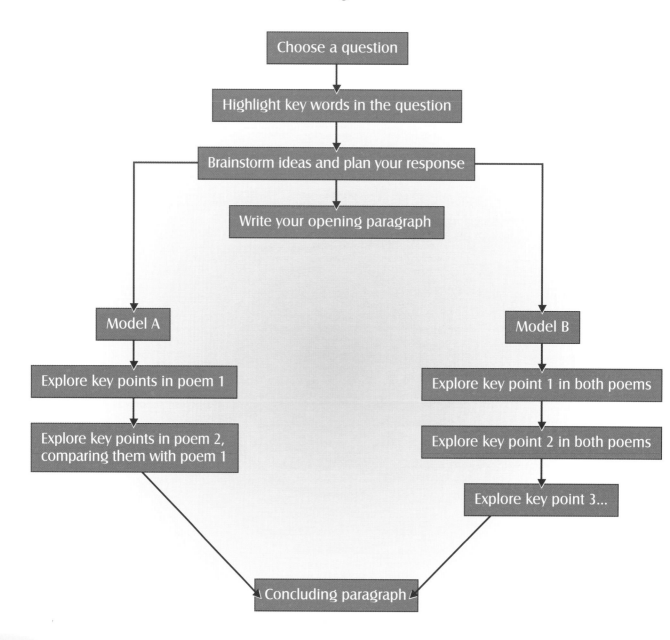

Choosing the question

There will be a choice of questions. Look carefully at the key words in each question and think about which poems you know well that could be used in a response.

1   **Highlighting key words**

It is important to have a clear focus in your response. Highlighting *key words* is an important stage in your planning and will help you select the two poems you will write about.

Here is an example of the kind of question you will be asked, with the key word highlighted.

Compare Half-Caste with one other poem, showing how poets reveal their ideas and feelings about aspects of the particular culture they are writing about. You should write about:

- what their ideas are
- what their feelings are
- the methods they use to reveal their ideas and feelings.

2   **Brainstorming ideas and planning (5–10 minutes)**

Half-Caste

> - main idea – it is ridiculous to label someone as 'half' something. People who do so aren't thinking clearly.
> - feelings – a mixture of amusement, disbelief, sarcasm
> - how? – unusual use of language/variety of metaphors/'loose' structure but a lot of rhyme and repetition

Two Scavengers in a Truck

> - main idea – American society, despite being democratic, is full of inequality (just as those labelled 'half-caste' are not treated as 'equal').
> - feelings – not as 'up front' as Half-Caste; more restrained. Some subtle criticism
> - how? – also uses metaphor/some American slang but largely standard English/no rhyme – a 'loose' structure.

3 Writing the opening paragraph

Let the examiner know from the outset what you are planning to do. You might begin:

> In 'Half-Caste', John Agard explores his ideas and feelings about use of the word 'half-caste' to describe people of mixed-race: he feels that it is wrong to treat them in what he considers to be a disrespectful way. 'Two Scavengers in a Truck' is set in a very different culture but also explores a writer's feelings and ideas about the differences between people.

The purpose of this opening is to indicate the two selected poems and to give some idea of the connection between them.

4 Model A

If you decide to write about each poem in turn, here is how the response to **Half-Caste** might develop as you focus on the 'ideas'. ▶

When you write about each poem in turn in Model A it is very important *to make points of comparison as you explore the second poem.*
To do this you will need to be able to use a range of words and phrases that are suitable for comparison, for example:

> whereas   on the other hand
> unlike   similarly   whilst
> alternatively   also   in contrast to

The point – The main idea is that it is wrong to describe someone whose parents are of different races as 'half' something. He uses a number of examples to develop this idea.

Supporting textual reference — The first example is a painter:

> 'yu mean when picasso
> mix red an green
> is a half-caste canvas/'

Developing the point — He is making the point that no one considers the mixing of colours as something that leads to a half colour: mixing colours leads to a new colour. It is interesting that he uses a very famous and important artist to make his point; it is almost as though he is saying that people of mixed race are special – just like Picasso was special.

Here are some examples of how to make points of comparison.

> While 'Half-Caste' is a quite dramatic poem with two voices, the only voice in 'Two Scavengers' is the poet's.

> Unlike 'Half-Caste', which is very much first-person poem, 'Two Scavengers' takes a third-person approach: there is no 'I' in the poem.

> The poet's feelings about his subject matter are far more obvious in 'Half-Caste' whereas in 'Two Scavengers'...

5 Model B

Following this approach, you write about both poems at the same time. In response to each key word – 'ideas', 'feelings' and 'methods' – you *compare* the poems. Here is an example of how you might write about 'the methods'.

> The poets explore ideas and express their feelings in very different ways. While John Agard has a very 'dramatic' and direct approach in which there is a speaker present in the poem, Ferlinghetti is more descriptive. The speaker in Agard's poem is very assertive and insistent:
>
>> 'Explain yuseif
>> wha yu mean
>> when yu say half-caste.'
>
> Whereas the poet's voice in 'Two Scavengers' is more reflective and calm:
>
>> 'And both scavengers gazing down
>>   as from a great distance
>>   at the cool couple.'
>
> Despite these different approaches, it is interesting that neither poet uses conventional punctuation, relying on line breaks to control the flow of words.

6 Ending the response

A good ending should draw points together and finish the piece of writing with something that sums up the response to the original question. Avoid simply repeating things you have already said. Here is how it could end:

> The two poems are clearly very different in subject matter and in their approach, but both are rooted in their particular cultures and both are about people and the ways their lives are influenced by the culture they live in.

POINTS TO REMEMBER

! Highlighting key words in questions helps you answer a question in a focused way.

! Select textual references which support your main points.

! There are different ways of writing about two poems but you should use appropriate vocabulary which shows you are comparing them.

How to approach Paper 2 Section A

In your examination you will be given a choice of **two** questions. You must answer **one** of these. You will have 45 minutes to plan and write your answer.

It will help you to:

- Consider **both** questions carefully. Think about which poems you would choose for both questions before you make your choice.
- Highlight key words in the question.
- Brainstorm ideas about the poems that are relevant to the question and then organise these.
- Make a note of quotations you might use.
- Re-read the question before starting to write.
- Re-read what you have written after every paragraph to make sure you are answering the question.
- Show your understanding of the poems through developed and insightful comments.

You are now ready to do your exam practice. Your teacher will tell you whether to answer the Foundation Tier or Higher Tier questions.

Exam Practice Foundation Tier

Answer **one** question in this Section.

Spend about **45 minutes** on this Section.

Either

1 Compare the ways in which the poets describe a place in **Two Scavengers in a Truck** and **one** other poem.

Write about:

- what the places are like
- how the language brings out what the places are like
- what you learn about the places from the people in them
- what the poets seem to think about the places
- what you think about the places.

Or

2 Compare what you are shown about conflict between cultures in **Half-Caste** with what you are shown about conflict between cultures in **one** other poem.

Write about:

- what you find out about the different cultures
- what the poets feel about the different cultures
- how the poets show their feelings to you.

Exam Practice Higher Tier

Answer **one** question in this Section.

Spend about **45 minutes** on this Section.

Either

1 Compare the ways in which the poets describe a place in **Two Scavengers in a Truck** and **one** other poem.

Or

2 Compare what you are shown about conflict between cultures in **Half-Caste** with what you are shown about conflict between cultures in **one** other poem.

The examiner comments ...

Now that you have studied two poems closely, you need to think about how you can apply what you have learnt to the other poems in your **Anthology**. During your English course you will be studying several poems from the clusters on *Different Cultures*. Use the following Assessment Objectives to help you to look at other poems.

Reading with insight and engagement

- Ask yourself questions about the meaning of the poem: Who? What? Where? When? Why? How?
- Are there other meanings buried beneath the surface?
- Are there significant symbols or images? How are they used? What do they mean?
- What is the mood or tone of the poem?
- Can you work out the attitude of the poet?

Making appropriate references to the text

- Which words, phrases or lines have particular significance?
- Are any words or phrases repeated for particular effect?
- How might you use these when writing about the poem?

Understanding and evaluating linguistic devices

- How does the writer use words to create particular images or to convey specific ideas or moods?
- What phrases can you select to exemplify these?
- How effective are these images?

Understanding structural and presentational devices

- What can you say about the way the words are set out on the page?
- Is there a link between presentation and content?
- How are the ideas organised?
- Is rhyme or repetition used? If so, how, and what is its effect?
- Is the rhythm regular or irregular? What is its effect?

Developing and sustaining your interpretation

- What did you think of the poem when you first read it?
- How have your views changed after looking at it more closely?
- Is there a bigger picture?
- Are there other ways of interpreting the poem?

Section B: *Writing to Inform, Explain or Describe*

In your exam you will be given a choice of writing tasks which require you to inform, explain or describe. Some of these tasks may be linked to themes in the **Anthology** poems studied for Section A.

You will be assessed on your ability in three areas:

Communication

You need to:

- state your ideas clearly and imaginatively
- adapt your writing for different purposes and readers
- be able to write in different forms, for example, a letter.

Organisation

You need to:

- organise your ideas into sentences, paragraphs and whole texts
- use a varied and appropriate vocabulary range
- use a variety of structural features, for example, a decisive ending.

Accuracy

You need to:

- use appropriate grammatical structures
- punctuate your writing accurately
- spell words correctly.

The emphasis in this section is on the ability to write in a more *personal and/ or descriptive* way. In the following pages we look at:

- examples of the different types of writing you will be asked to do
- the ways you should use the skills you have, and develop new skills.

1 Writing to inform

When you are writing to inform, your aim is to tell the reader about something or someone. This kind of writing appears in a variety of forms, such as autobiographies and biographies, travel writing, information leaflets, newspaper and magazine articles. The following extract is taken from a travel guide. In it the writer is informing the reader about music in the Caribbean.

  Activity **1**

Copy and complete this chart by finding evidence of the features of this article listed in the first column. Try to find more than one example if possible.

Features	Evidence of feature in the text
Range of information	Reggae, salsa, calypso, steel-band, less well-known forms; European, African, Indian and American and technological influences
Mixture of fact and opinion	
Use of rhetorical question to involve reader	
Addresses reader directly	
Use of technical terms relevant to subject	
Variety of sentence structures	
More sophisticated vocabulary choices	
Use of *cliché* (a frequently used and familiar phrase)	
Use of figurative language, e.g. a simile or metaphor	
Use of colloquial language, as normally found in casual speech	
Written in the present tense	

And the Beat Goes On

Caribbean music never stands still and the eastern islands, where fusion is a way of life, are fast earning a reputation as the music mecca of the world

Think of Caribbean music, and what do you come up with? Reggae would be an obvious first choice. Almost everybody can recognise the sound that took the world by storm in the 1970s with artists like Bob Marley and Peter Tosh and which is still a force to be reckoned with. And then what? Salsa became a phenomenon in the 1990s, with Cubans, Puerto Ricans and mainland Latin Americans setting the pace. Then there's calypso and steel-band, the infectious good-time music that seems to evoke the region in its every note.

But these three totally different types of music are just the tip of an ever-growing musical iceberg. Leaving aside the bigger islands, such as Jamaica, Cuba and Puerto Rico, even the smaller territories of the Lesser Antilles reveal an extraordinary diversity of styles and sounds that literally stretches from A to Z. In between Trinidad's aguinaldo and Martinique's zouk you'll find genres such as bélè (French islands), jing ping (Dominica), raggasoca (Barbados) and tambu (Dutch islands). And that's not to mention bouyon, parang and soukous.

Medley of influences

This baffling array of musical forms is testimony to the creativity and individuality of each Caribbean island. It also reminds us of the many different influences – linguistic as well as musical – which have left their mark on the region. European colonisers from Britain, France and Spain brought their music and instruments with them, recalled today in dances such as the *quadrille* of Martinique and Guadelope. From Africa came the drum-based rhythms and tradition of collective participation that underlie almost all contemporary styles in the region. Indian migrants contributed distinctive instruments and harmonies, especially in multicultural Trinidad. More recently, American jazz, rock'n'roll and rap have been incorporated and adapted into local forms, together with everything else from Latin brass sections to country and western.

Caribbean music never stands still. Constantly borrowing and developing, it keeps pace with technological advances while remaining rooted in age-old traditions. In a region where so many cultural influences, good and bad, have been absorbed, fusion is a way of life. No wonder that the Caribbean is fast earning a reputation as the music mecca of the world.

Another feature of the writing in **And the Beat Goes On** is its structure.

1 The article starts with a heading. What is suggested by the use of the word 'And' at the beginning of the heading?

2 Before the article starts properly there is a single sentence written in italics. This is called the 'lead'. What is its purpose?

3 Re-read the opening paragraph. In what ways does it:
   • draw the reader in
   • make the readers feel they know something about the subject
   • place the subject in a historical context?

4 The paragraphs are coherently linked. To trace the links between the paragraphs, answer these questions:
   a The second paragraph starts 'But these three totally different types of music ...' What are the three types of music? Where are they first mentioned?
   b The third paragraph starts 'This baffling array of musical forms ...' What is the baffling array of musical forms being referred to? Where are they first mentioned?
   c The fourth paragraph starts 'Caribbean music never stands still. Constantly borrowing and developing ...' Which countries have contributed to the development of Caribbean music? Where are they first mentioned?

Notice how points mentioned in one paragraph are developed or continued in the next.

Activity 3

Write the opening two paragraphs of an informative article on a subject in which you are interested. They could be about sport, fashion, a type of music or something else. Work through the following steps:

1 Brainstorm ideas connected to your chosen subject.

2 Decide which of these to include in your first and second paragraphs. Number them.

3 Look back at Activity 1 to remind yourself of some of the features of this type of *writing to inform*. Choose *at least* five of these features to include in your own writing and list them.

4 Note down your ideas on how to:
   • start your first paragraph
   • link your second paragraph to your first paragraph.

5 Write out your two paragraphs and redraft them carefully.

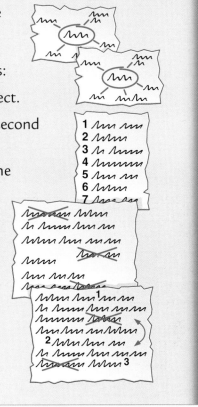

Informative writing can also be more personal. It can be about a significant incident or person in your life, or about a particular occasion, such as a school outing or a time when you made a serious mistake. This kind of writing is based on personal experience and is often found in biography and autobiography.

In the following extract from Maya Angelou's autobiography, she writes about her brother Bailey and makes clear his importance to her.

Activity 4

We learn about Bailey from what the writer tells us about:
• his appearance
• the things he does and says
• the way others react to him.

Summarise briefly what you learn about him in:
• lines 1 to 13
• lines 14 to 29
• lines 35 to 50
• lines 51 to 68
• lines 69 to 85.

I Know Why the Caged Bird Sings

by Maya Angelou

Bailey was the greatest person in my world. And the fact that he was my brother, my only brother, and I had no sisters to share him with, was such good fortune that it made me want to live a Christian life just to show God that I was grateful. Where I was big, elbowy and grating, he was small, graceful and smooth. When I was described by our playmates as being shit color, he was lauded for his velvet-black skin. His hair fell down in black curls, and my head was covered with black steel wool. And yet he loved me.

When our elders said unkind things about my features (my family was handsome to a point of pain for me), Bailey would wink at me from across the room, and I knew that it was a matter of time before he would take revenge. He would allow the old ladies to finish wondering how on earth I came about, then he would ask, in a voice like cooling bacon grease, 'Oh Mizeriz Coleman, how is your son? I saw him the other day and he looked sick enough to die.'

Aghast, the ladies would ask, 'Die? From what? He ain't sick.'

And in a voice oilier than the one before, he'd answer with a straight face, 'From the Uglies.'

I would hold my laugh, bite my tongue, grit my teeth and very seriously erase even the touch of a smile from my face. Later, behind the house by the black-walnut tree, we'd laugh and laugh and howl.

Bailey could count on very few punishments for his consistently outrageous behavior, for he was the pride of the Henderson/Johnson family.

His movements, as he was later to describe those of an acquaintance, were activated with oiled precision. He was also able to find more hours in the day than I thought existed. He finished chores, homework, read more books than I and played the group games on the side of the hill with the best of them. He could even pray out loud in church, and was apt at stealing pickles from the barrel that sat under the fruit counter and Uncle Willie's nose.

Once when the Store was full of lunchtime customers, he dipped the strainer, which we also used to sift weevils from meal and flour, into the barrel and fished for two fat pickles. He caught them and hooked the strainer onto the side of the barrel where they dripped until he was ready for them. When the last school bell rang, he picked the nearly dry pickles out of the strainer, jammed them into his pockets and threw the strainer behind the oranges. We ran out of the Store. It was summer and his pants were short, so the pickle juice made clean streams down his ashy legs, and he jumped with his pockets full of loot and his eyes laughing a 'How about that?' He smelled like a vinegar barrel or a sour angel.

After our early chores were done, while Uncle Willie or Momma minded the Store, we were free to play the children's games as long as we stayed within yelling distance. Playing hide-and-seek, his voice was easily identified, singing, 'Last night, night before, twenty-four robbers at my door. Who all is hid? Ask me to let them in, hit 'em in the head with a rolling pin. Who all is hid?' In follow the leader, naturally he was the one who created the most daring and interesting things to do. And when he was on the tail of the pop the whip, he would twirl off the end like a top, spinning, falling, laughing, finally stopping just before my heart beat its last, and then he was back in the game, still laughing.

Of all the needs (there are none imaginary) a lonely child has, the one that must be satisfied, if there is going to be hope and a hope of wholeness, is the unshaking need for an unshakable God. My pretty Black brother was my Kingdom Come.

Such informative descriptions help to make this account both lively and interesting. Of course it is not just what Maya Angelou says about her brother that is important. This is personal writing and reveals much about the writer herself. In the first paragraph, for example, the reader learns about:

- the writer's beliefs
- the way she feels about her appearance.

Re-read the passage and make notes on what you learn about Maya Angelou.

Activity 6

The effectiveness of a piece of writing depends largely on the way the writer expresses ideas. Maya Angelou's language is filled with imagery, which gives it vitality and interest. Copy and complete the following chart to show how the images work:

The image	What is the effect?	How is the effect achieved?
my head was covered black steel wool	Helps the reader to visualise the hair as wiry and very tightly curled	Through the use of metaphor – writer says something (hair) was something else (black steel wool)
in a voice like cooling bacon grease		
His movements … were activated with oiled precision.		
He smelled like a vinegar barrel or a sour angel.		
he would twirl off the end like a top, spinning, falling, laughing		
My pretty Black brother was my Kingdom Come.		

Writing your own

Choose one of your relatives to write about. Your aim is to tell your reader about this person. Use the structure below to help you.

Step 1 Gather ideas

First jot down ideas in response to the following prompts:

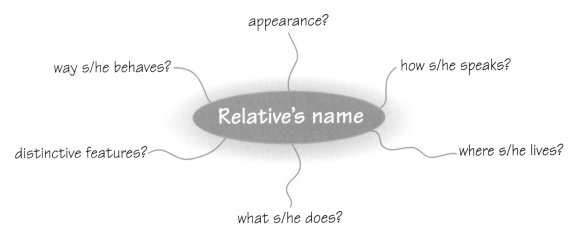

Step 2 Make brief notes on:

- an incident which would show what s/he is like
- your own feelings towards this person.

Step 3 Organise your ideas

Work out the order of ideas you are going to follow. You could use a similar structure to that used by Maya Angelou, or one of the following alternatives:

- *Time-based:* show how the person has changed and developed over a number of years. This might be a useful way to write about a younger brother or sister.
- *Photograph:* focus on the person at a particular time and place. This could work well if you are writing about someone who is now dead, perhaps a grandparent.
- *Contrast:* show the person in two or more very different situations, e.g. after a hard day's work and on holiday. This is one way of revealing the different roles of a person such as a parent.

These are only some of the options. You could find other ways of structuring your writing.

Step 4 Think about:

- the impression you want to give. What tone(s) should you adopt to achieve this e.g. humorous? serious? affectionate?
- how to use language to convey your ideas to your reader. What images would be appropriate? Should direct speech be included?
- your opening and ending. Look back at the Maya Angelou passage and consider the close connection between 'Bailey was the greatest person in my world' and 'My pretty Black brother was my Kingdom Come'.

Step 5 Plan your writing

You are now ready to plan your writing in more detail. Work out which details you are going to include and the order in which they will appear.

Your plan might look something like this:

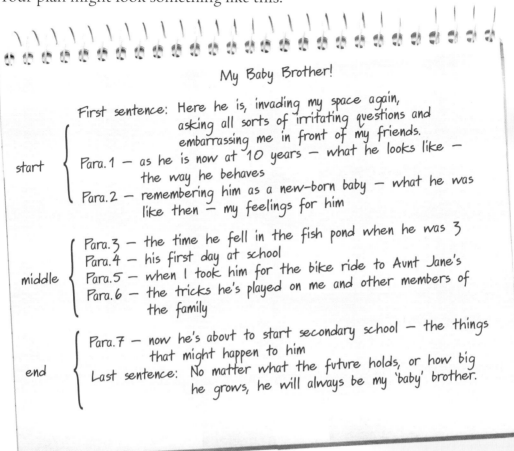

My Baby Brother!

start
{
First sentence: Here he is, invading my space again, asking all sorts of irritating questions and embarrassing me in front of my friends.

Para.1 — as he is now at 10 years — what he looks like — the way he behaves

Para.2 — remembering him as a new-born baby — what he was like then — my feelings for him
}

middle
{
Para.3 — the time he fell in the fish pond when he was 3

Para.4 — his first day at school

Para.5 — when I took him for the bike ride to Aunt Jane's

Para.6 — the tricks he's played on me and other members of the family
}

end
{
Para.7 — now he's about to start secondary school — the things that might happen to him

Last sentence: No matter what the future holds, or how big he grows, he will always be my 'baby' brother.
}

Step 6 Now you are ready to write

Remember, you will be assessed on *the way* that you write about the given subject. Your aim should be to make your writing as interesting and effective as you can.

> ### POINTS TO REMEMBER !
>
> ! When *writing to inform* your aim is to tell the reader about something or someone.
>
> ! Aim to organise your ideas into *coherently linked paragraphs*.
>
> ! Informative writing can be *personal* and sometimes reveals much about the writer.
>
> ! The *effectiveness* of your writing depends largely on the way you express your ideas.
>
> ! Aim to make your writing both *lively and interesting*.

2 Writing to explain

If a teacher asks you at school why you have done something, he or she is not asking for an account of what you have done but for an explanation as to *why* you have done it. You might also be asked to explain *how* something is done or *what* the effect of something might be.

One difficulty students sometimes have when writing to explain is in developing their ideas in sufficient detail. In the following article, Matthew Bridgeman explains how he developed an interest in running.

Activity

The following annotations highlight *the way* Matthew develops his explanation. As you read, match the annotations to the appropriate line numbers. The first one has been done for you:

Introduces subject by showing contrast between past and present: lines 1–12

Explains why and how he started to run:

Extends focus to look closely at diet:

Focuses on significant turning point:

Moves to present to emphasise progress:

Extends focus to explain how progress was made:

Gives examples of unfortunate experiences:

Highlights main achievement:

Concludes by looking to the future:

How to go from FAT to FIT

A little less than a year ago I was a tubby 14-year-old, feeding on chips and chocolate bars. My idea of exercise was changing TV channels by remote control. Now I am a lean 15-year-old, who eats baked potatoes and natural crunch bars, with a regular training schedule.

One day I found myself glued to the 'box', watching an international athletics meeting at Gateshead. It looked so much fun. All those strong athletes coasting around a 400-metre track at high speed. So, I thought I would have a go at it. The next day was warm and sunny with just a little light breeze. I donned my tracksuit bottoms, school athletics vest and best trainers, and I set off on a one-mile run. It was not as bad as I thought it was going to be and it took me just under eight minutes.

The next day was a different matter. I was as stiff as a board and I could hardly

continues overleaf

kneel down! But I went out again. And again and again. The stiffness went away and I did nothing but improve. After about two weeks I started doing two miles a day. Then 2.5 miles and 3 miles, gradually building up my stamina.

I decided to cut out all that excess sugar and fat from my diet. It didn't feel like 'slimming' because I wasn't eating less, just eating differently. I became a 'health fooder'. Porridge oats for breakfast, wholemeal bread in my lunch-box, chilli beans for dinner. It all seemed very filling! I drank just as much milk as before, only now it was skimmed milk. And I ate fresh fruit and yoghurt instead of cakes and puddings. Already I was feeling fitter and looking better.

Three and a half months after I started training I had a talk with one of my dad's friends who was a running coach. He told me that my running was lacking two factors: SPEED and STRENGTH. Also, the fact that I didn't have any rest days wasn't good for me or my running. He gave me a training programme which I have basically followed ever since.

My schedule has changed a lot since the early days when every day was a 2.5 mile run. The times have changed a lot too. I would have taken about 17 minutes to get round that 2.5 mile circuit then. Now it would take me under 12.30.

Just after Christmas, to strengthen my arms and legs, and for more sprinting power, I took up light weight-training using dumb-bells. I've read lots of articles which claim that weight-training is bad for your body if your body is still growing. But I think that if you are pretty fit, and do not use too heavy weights, it will help your running a lot. I never lift anything over 20 kgs at any one time. Then, at half-term I got a weight-bench and bar-bell. The weight-bench has leg-extension attachments, and the use of these in my training has really put muscles onto my legs.

My running has had its good and bad days, sad and funny days. There was the day I ran off the road onto the beach to find that the tide had come in. It was a very high tide. I had to run knee-deep in water for over two miles! I remember one particularly bad day when I did a cross-country run in deep snow and I seemed to be more on my bum than on my feet. That experience taught me not to run in deep snow again.

The obsession called 'NOT MISSING TRAINING' can be dangerous! Sad days are when you get sick or injured and cannot run. This winter I had a chest cold which stopped my running for a whole week! But every runner has good days. These are the days when everything goes right, you feel great, and you set a personal best: like last Wednesday, when I ran 38.30 for my five-mile training run in the rain.

It's always said that it's helpful to have some target to attain. So, I hope to see you at the Olympics!

Matthew Bridgeman

Now you are going to do the planning for this task, following the steps below:

Write about an interest that you have, explaining how that interest has developed and its importance to you.

1 Choose your subject

It may be that a particular interest springs to mind straight away. If so, write it down. If not, here are some suggestions for the kind of thing you could write about:

- a sport
- animals
- drama
- a school subject

- fashion
- reading
- a hobby

- music
- a club
- foreign travel

- art
- dancing
- computer games

2 Gather ideas

Once you have chosen your subject you need to generate some ideas. Make brief notes in answer to the following questions:

- When and how did you first become interested in this?
- What does the interest involve?
- How much time do you give to it?
- What do you enjoy about it?
- Are there any drawbacks?
- Have you made new friends through it?
- Has anything funny or odd happened because of it?
- Will it have any influence on your future?

3 Plan your writing

Now you are ready to start planning your writing. Decide:

- what you are going to write
- the order in which you are going to write.

You could organise your ideas around sub-headings, which could later be replaced with paragraphing, for example:

Football

- When I first became interested
- My favourite football club
- Details about the game
- A typical home match
- Me as a player
- Away games

Make your own sub-headings for your chosen subject. Under each sub-heading write brief notes on the details you will include. Then arrange your sub-headings into the order in which you will present them to your readers.

Now your plan is complete and you are ready to start writing.

 Activity 3

So far you have focused on how a writer develops ideas. Some other features of the writing in **How to go from fat to fit** are shown in the first column of the chart below. Look back at the article and write down at least one more example of each of these features:

Feature of writing	Example of feature	Other examples of features
The use of connectives that link cause and effect	It looked so much fun. All those strong athletes coasting around a 400-metre track at high speed. **So**, I thought I would have a go at it.	
The use of connectives that signal time	**After about two weeks** I started doing two miles a day.	
The use of capital letters for emphasis	He told me that my running was lacking two factors: **SPEED** and **STRENGTH**.	
The use of exclamation marks to stress significance	It all seemed very filling!	

Good writing is interesting writing. It is as much the way you write about something, as what you actually have to say, that makes a piece worth reading. In the following passage the writer explains through examples what it is like to live in an all-male household.

You know what the seven dwarfs were like before Snow White turned up?

We are a father and two sons living in a household without women. We are like an experiment in a satellite, free of normal earthly influences (like guilt, and bleach, and sock drawers). We've lived for years now in a whole new, all-male institution. Given its inadequacies as a child-rearing unit, I like it. It's so different from a household run by a woman. It's home alone except there are three of us. Here are a few characteristic gender moments:

One: Hugo is the most fastidious family member. He was holding one of our two little dogs. These are the only female elements in the house (and even then they poop all over the place). So: Hugo's holding one of the animals when it licks him. He looks around for a cloth and, realising he has both hands full with the animal, he lifts her up a bit and rubs her against his cheek. I say: 'Hugo. You just wiped your face with a *dog*.' That made me laugh and I thought it would do the same to his brother, this example of how unlike girls we were, but after asking which dog it was, Alexander made just one, rather irritable comment. He said: 'Why can't he wipe his face with his own dog!' This wasn't a plea for tolerance ('Why *can't* he wipe his face with his own dog!'), it was a protest against property abuse: ('Why can't he wipe his face with his *own* dog!').

Two: A naked six-year-old walks to the washing line in the early morning. It's late spring and one of those days when you know life is good. His rear end bobs between the plants and flowers; he climbs on a garden chair to select his wardrobe for the day. He spins the carousel to get at a T-shirt; he chooses the long navy-blue shorts; if he considers underpants he decides against them. And that's a blessing because it's one less thing to process. When I can get both of them to undress in front of the washing machine I'll have cut out several annoying links in the laundry chain. Using the washing line as a hanging rail eases a lot of pressure and this is why summer has been so important. It's allowed the evolution of a dressing system that doesn't distress and depress us. What I'm trying to ignore is the fact that summer doesn't last all year.

Three: I'm driving Alexander down a dusty beach road to the pie cart. A woman waiting on the bank takes one look at us and loses control – so much so I assume she's on drugs (or perhaps she's *not* on drugs – keeping up your medication isn't as easy as it sounds). 'What the *hell* do you think you're doing!' she cries. She's doing the voice that only angry mothers can do, it sounds like a power saw biting into timber. No, it sounds like one of those kung-fu fighting cries; it's like someone throwing a javelin into your ear. It's a voice that frightens Alexander far more than anything we've been doing driving round the park; and actually, because this voice goes to the roots of men, it rather frightens me too. Suddenly, both of us are five years old.

'*Get* that child off your windscreen,' she shrieks, 'you *bloody* fool!' We're driving at ten kilometres

50 an hour and Alexander is sitting on the windscreen; she assumes he's in danger. But what danger she sees that I don't is unclear.

He's holding on to one of the windscreen wipers, he's got both feet firmly on the middle of the bonnet, what's the problem? And it seemed it wasn't just a woman thing because her husband comes up to the car to add his voice to hers. 'You're
55 *crazy*,' he says. 'You irresponsible *fool*!'

I suppose in marriage you have to support your spouse. 'Back me up!' we say, whenever we say or we do something indefensible, like making children turn off *The Simpsons* because it's dinner time, or shrieking at amiable strangers peacefully driving their sons on the bonnet of their car.
60 Two years later I had devised the perfect retort to them both. I should have drawn myself up to my full height, as you are supposed to do in these situations, and said: 'Bite me.' That would have taught Alexander how to stick up for himself without being offensive. That's one of the most important lessons in life.

The Boys Are Back in Town by Simon Carr

Activity 4

1 Using examples is one way of developing *informative writing*. Simon Carr uses examples to show what life is like in an all-male household. Make notes on what you learn about life in an all-male household from these examples. Below are some prompts to help you:

Example 1 (lines 7 to 17) Talk about:	Example 2 (lines 18 to 31) Talk about:	Example 3 (lines 32 to 63) Talk about:
• Hugo's action • the father's reaction • Alexander's actions.	• Alexander's actions • the father's explanation.	• what they are doing • how they react to the tone of the woman's voice? • the different ways of seeing danger,

2 Carr uses a wide range of punctuation to present his examples clearly and to emphasise the humour of them. Examine the use of punctuation in the **first** example by completing the chart below:

Type of punctuation	Examples	Effects of punctuation
colon	One: So: I say: He said:	Gives the events a clear order – almost like a list
brackets		

Now repeat the exercise for the third example.

Writing your own

You are going to use the previous extract as a model to help you explain, through examples, what it is like to live in your *own* household. Work through the following steps:

1 Re-read the opening paragraph (lines 1–6). Notice how the writer clearly states:

- who lives in the household
- what is different about the way they live
- what he feels about it.

Write your own opening paragraph to include these points about *your* household.

2 Make notes about two or three examples that say something specific about the household in which you live. These might be to do with:

- a particular custom, e.g. mealtimes
- a shared reaction, e.g. how we feel about Aunt Agatha
- a family trait, e.g. excessive tidiness or short-temperedness
- a characteristic of one person, e.g. Dad's awful T-shirts, the way Gran always drinks too much at Christmas.

3 Aim to make your examples interesting and amusing by exaggerating a particular point or by including some revealing direct speech or using punctuation to enhance meaning. Each example must contain enough detail to explain something about your household.

4 Before writing, re-read the whole passage from **The Boys Are Back in Town** to remind you of what you are aiming for.

5 Now you are ready to write. Remember, you will be assessed on *the way* that you write about the given subject. Your aim should be to make your writing as interesting and effective as you can.

POINTS TO REMEMBER

! When you *write to explain* you give answers to How? and Why?
! Aim to *develop the detail* in your explanation.
! Ask yourself *questions* to generate ideas.
! Use *examples* to illustrate the points you want to make.
! Use *punctuation* to enhance meaning.
! Focus on making your writing *more interesting and/or amusing* for your reader.

3 Writing to describe

When writing to describe, you are trying to paint a picture with words. Your aim is to give your reader a clear picture of the person, place or scene that you are describing. One of the best ways to improve your skills in descriptive writing is to look at descriptions written by other writers and identify the features that make them effective.

Describing a person

Writers can use a range of techniques when describing people. In the following passage, the narrator, Scout, and her brother Jem are visiting an old lady, Mrs Dubose. Read the text through carefully, then go back and answer the questions that surround it.

What view is made clear in this simple statement?

What simile is used here? What is its effect?

Why has the writer used 'pinpoint'?

What does this reveal about the narrator's feelings?

What idea is repeated here?

What is suggested by the use of 'undulate'?

What is the effect of this metaphor?

What colour does this conjure up?

Why do you think the writer used the verb 'glistened'?

Imitate this action. Is the description accurate?

What change in the narrator's actions is emphasised in this single sentence paragraph?

Identify the two similes used. What images does each one create?

She was horrible. Her face was the colour of a dirty pillow-case, and the corners of her mouth glistened with wet, which inched like a glacier down the deep grooves enclosing her chin. Old-age liver spots dotted her cheeks, and her pale eyes had black pinpoint pupils. Her hands were knobbly, and the 5 cuticles were grown up over her finger-nails. Her bottom plate was not in, and her upper lip protruded; from time to time she would draw her nether lip to her upper plate and carry her chin with it. This made the wet move faster.

I didn't look any more than I had to. Jem reopened *Ivanhoe* 10 and began reading. I tried to keep up with him, but he read too fast. When Jem came to a word he didn't know, he skipped it, but Mrs Dubose would catch him and make him spell it out. Jem read for perhaps twenty minutes, during which time I looked at the soot-stained mantelpiece, out the window, 15 anywhere to keep from looking at her. As he read along, I noticed that Mrs Dubose's corrections grew fewer and farther between, that Jem had even left one sentence dangling in mid-air. She was not listening.

I looked towards the bed. 20

Something had happened to her. She lay on her back, with the quilts up to her chin. Only her head and shoulders were visible. Her head moved slowly from side to side. From time to time she would open her mouth wide, and I could see her tongue undulate faintly. Cords of saliva would collect on her 25 lips; she would draw them in, then open her mouth again. Her mouth seemed to have a private existence of its own. It worked separate and apart from the rest of her, out and in, like a clam hole at low tide. Occasionally it would say, 'Pt,' like some viscous substance coming to a boil. 30

To Kill a Mockingbird by Harper Lee

In the passage you have just read, Harper Lee clearly wants her readers to feel repelled by Mrs Dubose. To achieve this she paints a grotesque picture.

Write two paragraphs describing an imagined or real person in a way that makes them repellent to the reader, following these steps:

- picture the person
- decide where they are going to be – they could be moving or in one place
- decide which aspect(s) of the person's appearance you are going to focus on
- jot down some useful words and phrases
- think of and make a note of two similes you could use
- now write your description.

Describing a place

Writers also use a range of techniques to describe places. In the following extract, Roald Dahl describes his first sighting of Dar es Salaam, in Tanzania, Africa.

1 The order in which Dahl describes what he sees is important. As you read, arrange the things he saw, as listed below, into the correct order:

coconut palms	breakers	casuarina trees
rowers	church steeple	rim of lagoon
domed mosque	waterfront	trees	beaches
canoes	jungle	the town of Dar es Salaam

2 How does this sequence help to re-create the impression of Dahl's 'first glimpse' of Dar es Salaam through the port-hole?

DAR ES SALAAM

When I woke up the next morning the ship's engines had stopped. I jumped out of my bunk and peered through the port-hole. This was my first glimpse of Dar es Salaam and I have never forgotten it. We were
5 anchored out in the middle of a vast rippling blue-black lagoon and all around the rim of the lagoon there were pale-yellow sandy beaches, almost white, and breakers were running up on to the sand, and coconut palms with their little green leafy hats were growing on the
10 beaches, and there were casuarina trees, immensely tall and breathtakingly beautiful with their delicate grey-green foliage. And then behind the casuarinas was what seemed to me like a jungle, a great tangle of tremendous dark-green trees that were full of shadows
15 and almost certainly teeming, so I told myself, with rhinos and lions and all manner of vicious beasts. Over to one side lay the tiny town of Dar es Salaam, the houses white and yellow and pink, and among the houses I could see a narrow church steeple and a
20 domed mosque and along the waterfront there was a line of acacia trees splashed with scarlet flowers. A fleet of canoes was rowing out to take us ashore and the black-skinned rowers were chanting weird songs in time with their rowing.
25   The whole of that amazing tropical scene through the port-hole has been photographed on my mind ever since. To me it was all wonderful, beautiful and exciting. And so it remained for the rest of my time in Tanganyika. I loved it all. There were no furled
30 umbrellas, no bowler hats, no sombre grey suits and I never once had to get on a train or a bus.

42

Going Solo by Roald Dahl

Activity 3

Identify other features of Roald Dahl's technique by answering these questions:

1 What is the effect of the very long fourth sentence (lines 4–12)? Why do you think Dahl started his next sentence with the conjunction 'And'?

2 List the different colours referred to in the extract. What is the effect of these?

3 Explain what effect has been created by :
- the use of adjectives in 'immensely tall and breathtakingly beautiful with their delicate grey-green foliage'. (lines 10–12)
- the images created in 'coconut palms with their little green leafy hats' (lines 8–9) and 'a great tangle of tremendous dark-green trees'. (lines 13–14)
- the choice of verb in 'a line of acacia trees splashed with scarlet flowers'. (line 21)
- the use of repetition in 'no furled umbrellas, no bowler hats, no sombre grey suits'. (lines 29–30)

Activity 4

Think of a place you know well and create a photograph of it in your mind. You are going to describe it for a reader, starting either:
- from the front of the photograph to the back

or
- from one side of the photograph to the other.

1 Start by making a note of the main features and colours in your 'photograph'.

2 Now make notes on ways you could use adjectives, images, verbs and repetition to help re-create your 'photograph'.

3 Think about how you could vary your sentence length to make your description more interesting.

4 Finally, write your description. Re-read it after every three sentences to make sure you are giving a clear picture of your 'photograph'. When you have finished writing, read through it carefully and make any last-minute changes and improvements.

In the extract from **Going Solo** Dahl presents the details of his first glimpse of Dar es Salaam in quick succession. The speed with which he relates these details helps to create the feelings of excitement and enthusiasm which he experienced at the time. By the end of the description he has re-created the photograph in his mind, so that the reader can see it in the same way as he did.

Describing a scene

When describing a scene you often need to consider both people and place. It is important to describe the scene in an organised way and to re-create its atmosphere.

In the following extract Michael Anthony describes an alley he knew as a child when living in San Fernando in Trinidad. Answer the questions as you read through the extract:

Enchanted Alley

1 Read lines 1–33. What is the focus of the first paragraph? What is the focus of the second paragraph? How does the writer link the two?

Leaving for school on mornings, I walked slowly through the busy parts of town. The business places would all be opening then and smells of strange fragrance would fill
5 the High Street. Inside the opening doors I would see clerks dusting, arranging, hanging things up, getting ready for the day's business. They looked cheerful and eager and they opened the doors
10 very wide. Sometimes I stood up to watch them.

In places between the stores several little alleys ran off the High Street. Some
15 were busy and some were not and there was one that was long and narrow

and dark and very strange. Here, too, the shops would be opening as I passed and 20 there would be bearded Indians in loincloths spreading rugs on the pavement. There would be Indian women also, with veils thrown over their shoulders, setting up their stalls and chatting 25 in a strange sweet tongue. Often I stood, too, watching them, and taking in the fragrance of rugs and spices and onions and sweetmeats. And 30 sometimes, suddenly remembering, I would hurry away for fear the school-bell 35 had gone.

2 How is the alley made to seem mysterious?
Now read lines 37–50.

In class, long after I settled down, the thoughts of this alley would return to me. I would recall certain stalls and certain beards and certain flashing eyes, and even some of the rugs that had been rolled out. The Indian women, too, with bracelets around their ankles and around their sun-browned arms flashed to my mind.

I thought of them. I saw them again looking shyly at me from under the shadow of the stores, their veils half hiding their faces. In my mind I could almost picture them laughing together and talking in that strange sweet tongue. And mostly the day would be quite old before the spell of the alley wore off my mind.

3 What words make the alley seem like a magical place? What effect does the alley have on the boy?
Now read lines 51–69.

4 What details does the writer include to increase the sense of mystery?

One morning I was much too early for school. I passed the street-sweepers at work on Harris' Promenade and when I came to the High Street, only one or two shop doors were open. I walked slowly, looking at the quietness and noticing some of the alleys that ran away to the backs of fences and walls and distant streets. I looked at the names of these alleys. Some were very funny. And I walked on anxiously so I could look a little longer at the dark, funny street.

As I walked it struck me that I did not know the name of that street. I laughed at myself. Always I had stood there looking along it and I did not know the name of it. As I drew near I kept my eyes on the wall of the corner shop. There was no sign on the wall. On getting there I looked at the other wall. There was a sign-plate upon it but the dust had gathered thickly there and whatever the sign said was hidden behind the dust.

Now read to the end of the passage.

5 The writer tells us much about the place through his reactions to it. Identify and list the different feelings he experiences in lines 70–116.

70 I was disappointed. I looked along the alley which was only now beginning to get alive, and as the shop doors opened the enchantment of spice and onions and sweetmeats emerged. I looked at the wall again but there was nothing there to say what the street
75 was called. Straining my eyes at the sign-plate I could make out a 'C' and an 'A' but farther along the dust had made one smooth surface of the plate and the wall.

'Stupes!' I said in disgust. I heard mild laughter, and as I looked before me I saw the man rolling out
80 his rugs. There were two women beside him and they were talking together and they were laughing and I could see the women were pretending not to look at me. They were setting up a stall of sweetmeats and the man put down his rugs and took
85 out something from a tray and put it into his mouth, looking back at me. Then they talked again in the strange tongue and laughed.

I stood there awhile. I knew they were talking about me. I was not afraid. I wanted to show them
90 that I was not timid and that I would not run away. I moved a step or two nearer the wall. The smells rose up stronger now and they seemed to give the feelings of things splendoured and far away. I pretended I was looking at the wall but I stole
95 glances at the merchants from the corners of my eyes. I watched the men in their loin-cloths and the garments of the women were full and many-coloured and very exciting. The women stole glances at me and smiled at each other and ate the sweetmeats
100 they sold. The rug merchant spread out his rugs wide on the pavement and he looked at the beauty of their colours and seemed very proud. He, too, looked slyly at me.

I drew a little nearer because I was not afraid of
105 them. There were many more stalls now under the stores. Some of the people turned off the High Street and came into this little alley and they bought little things from the merchants. The merchants held up the bales of cloth and matched them on to the
110 people's clothes and I could see they were saying it looked very nice. I smiled at this and the man with the rugs saw me and smiled.

That made me brave. I thought of the word I knew in the strange tongue and when I remembered
115 it I drew nearer.
'Salaam,' I said.

Best West Indian Stories by Michael Anthony

Looking at technique

The writer uses a range of techniques in his description of the alley.

He creates an *atmosphere of mystery* through the way he describes the scene:

'I saw them again looking shyly at me from under the shadow of the stores, their veils half hiding their faces.' (lines 44–6)

'The smells rose up stronger now and they seemed to give the feelings of things splendoured and far away.' (lines 91–3)

He uses *lists* and frequent *use of the conjunction 'and'* to help build up the detail. There are lists of:

nouns: '... and taking in the fragrance of rugs and spices and onions and sweetmeats.' (lines 28–30)

verbs: '... I would see clerks dusting, arranging, hanging things up, getting ready for the day's business.' (lines 6–8)

adjectives: '... and there was one that was long and narrow and dark and very strange.' (lines 16–19)

The writer uses a *range of sentence structures*, for example:

simple sentence that communicates and emphasises one idea ———— 'I was disappointed. I looked along the alley which ———— **complex** sentence that communicates more than one idea and offers a sequence of detail by using two or more clauses
was only now beginning to get alive, and as the shop doors opened the enchantment of spice and onions and sweetmeats emerged. I looked at the wall again but there was nothing there to say what the street was called.' (lines 70–5)

compound sentence that links two or more simple sentences to link or contrast information or ideas by using a conjunction such as 'but' or 'and'

This range of sentence structure provides variety and richness to the text.

Activity 5

1 Scan the text to find other examples of:
   - words and phrases used to create a sense of mystery
   - lists of words and phrases which help to build up the detail.

2 Identify what types of sentence are being used here. Why do you think the writer chose to use them?

   a 'I looked along the alley which was only now beginning to get alive, and as the shop doors opened the enchantment of spice and onions and sweetmeats emerged.' (lines 70–3)

   b 'I stood there awhile. I knew they were talking about me. I was not afraid.' (lines 88–9)

   c 'The rug merchant spread out his rugs wide on the pavement and he looked at the beauty of their colours and seemed very proud.' (lines 100–102)

Writing your own

When describing a scene your aim is to create a vivid picture of it for your reader. Use the steps below to help you to:

Describe a park on a summer's day

1 Gather as many ideas as you can by using your five senses. To do this make notes on what you can see, hear, taste, smell and feel.

2 Develop your ideas further. Look at the notes you've just made about what you can see. Perhaps you've included children playing, people walking or someone sunbathing. Start to build up a pool of descriptive words or phrases for each thing you have listed.

> e.g. children playing: excitedly, energetically, furiously, like bees buzzing, like prisoners on their first day of freedom.

Further ideas may come from this:

> e.g. one little boy in tattered T-shirt and shorts starts to cry helplessly.

Spend about five minutes generating ideas and words in this way.

3 Once the scene is clear in your mind, decide how to structure your description. You need to give your writing some point of focus, something that links the ideas together. Here are some suggestions of how you could do this:
   - follow one person, perhaps a little brother or sister, as they move around the park
   - you are waiting for someone – record your impressions as the minutes tick by
   - give the wider picture and then zoom in on one particular area.

4 When you start to write, aim to use some or all of the following:
   - words and phrases which help to create atmosphere
   - lists which help to build up detail
   - a range of sentence structures which gives variety and richness.

5 As you begin to write, remind yourself that your reader cannot see what is in your mind. It is up to you to choose the best words to paint your picture as clearly as you can.

POINTS TO REMEMBER

! When *writing to describe* you are trying to paint a picture with words.

! You need to use a *range of techniques* when describing people, places and scenes.

! Always *structure your ideas* carefully.

! Try to *describe the atmosphere* of a scene for your reader.

! Use a range of *vocabulary and sentence structures*.

How to approach Paper 2 Section B

In this section of the exam you are given a choice of **writing** tasks from which you should choose one. The types of writing tested here are writing which informs, explains or describes. In the exam they may be combined.

The exam questions on the following pages are sometimes linked thematically to the poetry used in the Section A Exam Practice papers (pages 135–6). The questions in Section B are usually the same in Foundation and Higher Tiers.

Making your choice and planning your ideas

Make sure you take time to think about which task to do. It is important that you:

• choose the task which gives you the opportunity to write well
• have plenty of ideas to write about.

Read all the options carefully and consider what you could write for each one.

Once you have made your choice, you are ready to start planning. In the exam you should spend about five minutes planning. For these practice questions it will probably take you longer than that.

Remember that the plan is for *your* benefit. It will help you produce a well-structured and interesting piece of writing. You will not be directly assessed on your plan in the exam but without it you are less likely to produce a good piece of writing. **The examiner comments** section on page 164 takes you through the stages you need to work through before starting to write your answer.

Exam Practice Foundation and Higher Tiers

Writing to inform, explain or describe

Answer **one** question in this Section.
Spend about **45 minutes** on this Section.

Remember:
- Spend about 5 minutes planning and sequencing your material
- Write about 1½ sides
- Spend about 5 minutes checking
  ✓ your paragraphing ✓ your punctuation ✓ your spelling.

Either

1 A student from another area is coming to stay with you. Write a letter **informing** him or her about:
- your home and your local area

and

- what you plan to do during the visit.

Or

2 Many writers recall important events in their lives and explain how these have affected them. Write about a significant event in your life and **explain** how it has affected you.

Or

3 Many people think it is important to have a room of their own to escape to. **Describe** the room that you would like to have.

Or

4 Write about a time when you wanted to, or actually did, leave home. **Explain** why you wanted to leave and **describe** your feelings at the time.

The examiner comments

This section is testing you on your ability to inform, explain or describe. Study the four stages described below carefully to help you achieve your best results in the exam.

1 Choosing

- Select your task carefully. Make sure you have plenty to write about. There is no point starting to write and after ten minutes finding you have nothing more to say.
- Remember that while the writing in this section is likely to draw on personal experience, it does not have to be entirely true. For example, in response to Question 1 you could write about an area you know well and pretend it was your home.

2 Planning

- Examiners report that students who plan carefully almost always achieve higher results than those who don't.
- Use the skills you have developed in the previous chapters of this book to help you gather and organise your ideas.
- Think of interesting opening and closing sentences that will appeal to your reader.

3 Writing

- Aim to express your ideas as clearly and effectively as you can. Look at the following examples:

> a) In the corner there would be my HiFi system. I love to listen to music but my room would have to be soundproofed so as not to disturb my Mum and Dad.
>
> b) My treasured HiFi would occupy the prime corner position. The room would, of course, be soundproofed so that I could turn up the volume and my tone-deaf parents could still watch EastEnders in peace!

They use the same subject matter yet b) is livelier, uses more adjectives and shows a stronger sense of audience through the use of 'of course' and the exclamation mark.

- Re-read what you have written after every paragraph. Research shows that students who do this stick to the subject, make fewer mistakes and achieve higher grades.

4 Checking

- A third of the marks will be awarded for accuracy in your use of grammar, your spelling and your punctuation. Be aware of areas in which you are most likely to make mistakes and double check these points.
- Try reading your work aloud mentally. Make sure you read the words on the page, not the words you think are on the page! This will help you to spot any errors in grammar and/or punctuation.

Sample paper 1 Foundation Tier

Time: 1 hour 45 minutes

Instructions to candidates:

- Answer **all** of Section A and **one question** from Section B.
- You must **not** use a dictionary in this exam.

Section A: Reading non-fiction and media texts

Answer **all** the questions in this Section.
Spend about **60 minutes** on this Section.

Read the non-fiction text, **A Letter to My Brother** and the media text,
Why Asians don't want to corner the market in shops any more.

1 Raj is writing this letter to her brother Jasmit.

- Read lines 4–9 closely. List three opinions from these lines that Jasmit has about Raj. **(3 marks)**
- List three opinions that Raj states about herself in lines 10–17. **(3 marks)**

2 Both writers use rhetorical questions. Copy one example of this from each text. For each one explain why the writer has used it. **(4 marks)**

3 **Why Asians don't want to corner the market in shops any more** is a media text. Write about:

- what you have found out about its intended purpose **and** its intended audience
- the way meaning is put across through the pictures it uses
- how the layout and presentation contribute to its effect. **(9 marks)**

4 Think about both texts and the arguments put forward by both writers. What does **each** text show you about:

- the changes taking place amongst British Asians **(4 marks)**
- the reasons for these changes? **(4 marks)**

A Letter to My Brother

Dear Jasmit

Thank you so much for pointing out what is so desperately wrong with my life, according to *your* narrow-minded views.

I can see that in your eyes, I am an emotionally unstable teenage Asian female, who knows nothing about her identity or culture. Do you know how many times I used to question my identity? It was a bit hard not to, when you were constantly pointing out that the colour of my skin was more 'white' than 'brown' and that I 'acted white'. According to you I was 'sad' because I didn't listen to bhangra music.

Well, let me tell you, just because I don't listen to bhangra, it doesn't mean that I am trying to adopt another culture. I'm not a sheep that follows what everyone else does, I'm an individual who has the right to make my *own* decisions.

For your information, I am not uncultured; our parents did a good job of bringing me up. I know what is morally wrong and right, I have morals, principles and opinions. I know how to speak my mother tongue and I wear my national dress.

You're always saying that I'll be lucky to get married and have children, the way I am. Is that what you think? That I will spend my life just as somebody's wife, with no identity of my own, content to look after the house and stay in the kitchen all day? Do you *really* think that all Asian wives need to keep them happy is a new microwave?

The answer is NO! I don't know which century you are living in, but I'm telling you one thing for sure – being an Asian woman is not a punishment or a restriction. The world is my oyster and my life will be what I make it!

Well, I'm writing to thank you! Because of all your narrow-minded ideas and scorn, I have become stronger and more independent. I am more determined than ever to get an education. I intend to get a decent job and spend my life comfortably, not dependent on any man. I want to be as free as possible and I want to be *me*, not an extension of someone else. I don't want to live my life in someone else's shadow.

I finally have enough confidence to speak out and say 'Yes, I'm a young Asian woman and I'm going to do something with my life!'

Your loving sister,

Raj

Telling it like it is, Livewire

Why Asians don't want to corner the market in shops any more

AMAR SINGH

A corner shop not far from where I grew up recently shut for good. As I drove past and saw this tiny institution closed on a weekday, for what seemed the first time ever, I remembered what it meant to me as a youngster.

It was a little island of my culture where Bollywood songs played on the radio and one of several family members would serve you in Hindi.

Against all odds. Asians who have found success away from the family business.

The owner's son is a friend of mine. He's never been interested in working 16 hours a day in what was once his family business so he's studying to be a lawyer.

According to research by Professor David McEvoy, of Liverpool's John Moores University, this is not unfamiliar. A combination of competition from supermarkets and petrol stations, in addition to a wave of young British Asians unwilling to work in the family business, is reportedly killing off the corner shop.

The institution referred to in the first episode of *EastEnders* as a 'Paki shop' will be missed by many. But if its end means that a new generation of Asians will move into less traditional sectors, then let the corner shop rest in peace. Fewer shopkeepers and more politicians, fewer restaurant owners and more civil servants? Why not?

Many Asians born here are benefiting from their parents' hard work and have been given the chance to study and pursue interests that previous generations never were.

The past few years have seen many British Asians excel in white-dominated professions or simply less typically 'Asian' careers. We still have great Asian businessmen, doctors and accountants but Britain's Asian community is now producing a heap of more widely talented individuals.

The comedy of the corner shop era has been defined by Meera Syal and the *Goodness Gracious Me* team. They have not only educated the ignorant but shown that Asians can poke fun at themselves too with the famous 'Going Out For An English' sketch, which featured rowdy Asian boozers in an English restaurant in India.

There are Asians making great progress in both the music and the fashion industries and there are a couple of football players on the verge of becoming the first British Asians to play in the Premiership.

Michael Chopra is a young striker who was handed a squad number by Newcastle boss Bobby Robson in October after he scored 14 goals in nine games for the club's Academy side. His dad's profession? A newsagent. So, one day there's a good chance that England supporters will be thankful that Michael decided he didn't want to work in the family business.

Section B: Writing to argue, persuade or advise

Answer **one** question in this Section.

Spend about **45 minutes** on this Section.

You may use some of the information from Section A (pages 165–7) if you want to, but you do not have to do so.

If you use any of the information do not simply copy it.

Remember:
- Spend about 5 minutes planning and sequencing your material
- Write at least 1½ sides in your answer book
- Spend about 5 minutes checking
  - ✓ your paragraphing   ✓ your punctuation   ✓ your spelling.

Either

5 We often feel that people have the wrong impression of us. Write a letter to someone who you feel has the wrong impression of you. It could be a relative, a teacher, a friend or someone else. Your aim is to challenge their view and **argue** against it. Remember to:
- make your key points clearly
- support your argument with evidence and examples.

Or

6 Education is often the route to better jobs and more choices. Your Head of Year is to give a speech in assembly to **persuade** pupils to make the most of the educational opportunities offered to them. Write the script for this speech.
  Remember to:
- give reasons why they should work hard at school
- choose the right language for a speech that persuades.

Or

7 Write an **advice** sheet for Year 11 students on: **How to make the most out of your life!** Remember to:
- offer a range of advice
- address your readers directly.

Or

8 Write an article for a student magazine on the subject of 'Career Choices'. Your aim is to **advise** students on a range of possible careers and to **persuade** them to think carefully about their choices.

Sample paper 1 Higher Tier

Time: 1 hour 45 minutes

Instructions to candidates:

- Answer **all** of Section A and **one question** from Section B.
- You must **not** use a dictionary in this exam.

Section A: Reading non-fiction and media texts

Answer **all** the questions in this Section.
Spend about **60 minutes** on this Section.

Read the non-fiction text, **When you don't feel like a foreigner** and the media text, **Why Asians don't want to corner the market in shops any more**.

1 How does the writer of **When you don't feel like a foreigner** feel about being an Asian in England? To answer this you will need to focus on her opinions.   **(6 marks)**

2 **Why Asians don't want to corner the market in shops any more** is a media text. What have you found out about:
   - its intended purpose and audience
   - how meaning is conveyed through pictures
   - how layout and presentation contribute to its effect?   **(9 marks)**

3 Think about both texts and the arguments put forward by both writers. What does each text show you about:
   - the problems faced by British Asians   **(4 marks)**
   - the changes taking place amongst British Asians   **(4 marks)**
   - the reasons for these changes?   **(4 marks)**

When you don't feel like a foreigner

It is never easy being a foreigner in a country; it is even more difficult when you don't feel like a foreigner.

I am an Asian girl, originally from India, though I was born here in England eighteen years ago. I live in relative comfort in an exceptionally nice area of the town with all the amenities and many of the luxuries at my disposal. I enjoy my life here and would find it difficult to imagine living in another country.

I think people in all spheres of life are bound to experience prejudice at one time or another, be it for their race, colour or creed but perhaps we Asians are subject to prejudice in all these areas. I have found that there are two main types of prejudice: the kind that is expressed in loud, explicit and often violent tones, the other a more subtle though no less expressive type. The former I do not experience directly very often and as yet never in its violent form. It is intimidating to have to walk past a group of young 'skinheads' and suffer being called names such as 'smelly paki' or 'chocolate drop' or have to cross the road to avoid a group of older 'skinheads'. I believe these human beings who look and sound as they do are as much a pest to English people as they are to us.

The second form of prejudice is the type I encounter from my good friends. My best friends are all English and white and when they use phrases like, 'I don't think of you as being an Indian, I mean you don't smell of curry or speak with an Indian accent', they often astonish me in their naivety at thinking that all Indians are like that.

Parental care, to all appearances, is much more protective and thus restrictive in Indian homes than English ones. From my own experience I find it extremely annoying, especially since my friends are not treated in the same way. My parents insist on knowing where I am when I go out, though not necessarily who I am with, what time I will be home and how I am getting home. Personally, I find this an overprotective part of my parents' nature, but of course, having spoken to many other Indian girls in my college, this constitutes complete freedom in comparison with them.

Marriage of course is a major topic of conversation for girls of my age, since within the next few years we all hope to be married. My friends find my marriage arrangements interesting because they are never sure whether or not a marriage is to be arranged for me. My views on this subject have changed over the years. Until a few years ago I felt arranged marriages to be very unromantic and I couldn't understand how couples could be content with this arrangement. I then began speaking to girls who considered an arranged marriage to be acceptable, in some cases even desirable. I now believe that, from reading recent statistics, 'love' marriages are not more successful than arranged marriages; however, I feel that it is the freedom of choice in a 'love' marriage that makes me covet one. I feel that I should have a complete choice in the man with whom I am to spend the rest of my life, the chance to make up my own mind about the person I could be happy with, the freedom to decide my future, be it the right or the wrong choice.

When you don't feel like a foreigner by Rita from *Community Writing,* edited by Don Shiach

Why Asians don't want to corner the market in shops any more

AMAR SINGH

A corner shop not far from where I grew up recently shut for good. As I drove past and saw this tiny institution closed on a weekday, for what seemed the first time ever, I remembered what it meant to me as a youngster.

It was a little island of my culture where Bollywood songs played on the radio and one of several family members would serve you in Hindi.

The owner's son is a friend of mine. He's never been interested in working 16 hours a day in what was once his family business so he's studying to be a lawyer.

According to research by Professor David McEvoy, of Liverpool's John Moores University, this is not unfamiliar. A combination of competition from supermarkets and petrol stations, in addition to a wave of young British Asians unwilling to work in the family business, is reportedly killing off the corner shop.

The institution referred to in the first episode of *EastEnders* as a 'Paki shop' will be missed by many. But if its demise means that a new generation of Asians will move into less traditional sectors, then let the corner shop rest in peace. Fewer shopkeepers and more politicians, fewer restaurant owners and more civil servants? Why not?

Britain's public sector is still a long way from representing our multicultural demography but the tide is turning. Many Asians born here are benefiting from their parents' enterprise against all the odds and have been given the chance to study and pursue interests that previous generations never were.

The past few years have seen many British Asians excel in white-dominated professions or simply less typically 'Asian' careers and these kinds of success stories now constitute a defining characteristic of 'Cool Britannia'. We still have great Asian businessmen, doctors, accountants and pharmacists but Britain's Asian community is now producing a heap of more talented individuals.

In music we've seen Talvin Singh and Nithin Sawnhey combine their knowledge and mastery of both Eastern musical discipline and Western beats to produce an authentically British Asian sound. Others such as Aki-Nawaz, of Fundamental and the Asian Dub Foundation,

Against all odds. Asians who have found success away from the family business.

have refused to let go of their culture but are determined to be heard. They sing and rap of racism but also celebrate having the best of both worlds by being British Asian.

The comedy of the corner-shop era has been defined by Meera Syal and the *Goodness Gracious Me* team, who have not only educated the ignorant but shown that Asians can poke fun at themselves too. They satirise racial prejudices and even turned them on their heads with the famous 'Going Out For An English' sketch, which featured rowdy Asian boozers in an English restaurant in India.

The fashion industry is no exception to this trend. Ruby Hammer, a beautician and internationally acclaimed make-up artist, is creating looks for some of the world's top designers and has formed Ruby and Millie, the first major UK cosmetics brand to launch in 30 years, with her friend Millie Kendall.

We all know the old joke. Why are Asians no good at football? Because every time they get a corner they build a shop. Well, there are a couple of football players on the verge of becoming the first British Asians to play in the Premiership.

Michael Chopra is a young striker who was handed a squad number by Newcastle boss Bobby Robson in October after he scored 14 goals in nine games for the club's Academy side. His dad's profession? A newsagent. So, one day there's a good chance that England supporters will be thankful that Michael decided he didn't want to work in the family business.

So, goodbye corner shop. Along with countless others I will miss your quirky and quaint ways but I will also look forward to a time when British Asians appear on the back page of the newspapers that you sell and on the front cover of the celebrity magazines that lie on your shelves.

Section B: Writing to argue, persuade or advise

Answer **one** question in this Section.

Spend about **45 minutes** on this Section.

You may use some of the information from Section A (pages 169–71) if you want to, but you do not have to do so.

If you use any of the information do not simply copy it.

Remember:
- Spend about 5 minutes planning and sequencing your material
- Try to write at least 1½ sides
- Spend about 5 minutes checking
  ✓ your paragraphing   ✓ your punctuation   ✓ your spelling.

Either

4 We often feel that people have the wrong impression of us. Write a letter to someone who you feel has the wrong impression of you. It could be a relative, a teacher, a friend or someone else. Your aim is to challenge their view and **argue** against it.

Or

5 Education is often the route to better jobs and more choices. Your Head of Year is to give a speech in assembly to **persuade** pupils to make the most of the educational opportunities offered to them. Write the script for this speech.

Or

6 Write an **advice** sheet for Year 11 students on: **How to make the most out of your life!**

Or

7 Write an article for a newspaper on the subject of prejudice in Britain. Your aim is to:
- **advise** readers on how to deal with prejudice
- **argue** for stronger laws to deal with prejudiced behaviour.

Sample paper 2 Foundation Tier

Time: 1 hour 30 minutes

Instructions to candidates:

- Answer **all** of Section A and **one question** from Section B.
- You must **not** use a dictionary in this exam.

Section A: Reading poems from different cultures and traditions

Answer **one** question in this Section.
Spend about **45 minutes** on this Section.

Either

1 Compare how the poets show you something important about the culture or cultures they are writing about in **Two Scavengers in a Truck** and **one** other poem.

Write about:
- what you are shown about the culture(s)
- how the language brings out what the culture(s) are like
- what the poets seem to think about the culture(s)
- what you think about the culture(s).

Or

2 Compare the ways in which the poets present people in **Half-Caste** and **one** other poem.

Write about:
- what you find out about the people
- the methods the poets use to show you the people
- similarities and differences between the methods the poets use.

Sample paper 2 Higher Tier

Time: 1 hour 30 minutes

Instructions to candidates:

- Answer **all** of Section A and **one question** from Section B.
- You must **not** use a dictionary in this exam.

Section A: Reading poems from different cultures and traditions

Answer **one** question in this Section.
Spend about **45 minutes** on this Section.

Either

1 Compare how the poets show you something important about the culture or cultures they are writing about in **Two Scavengers in a Truck** and **one** other poem.

Or

2 Compare the ways in which the poets present people in **Half-Caste** and **one** other poem.

Sample paper 2 Foundation and Higher Tiers

Section B: Writing to inform, explain or describe

Answer **one** question in this Section.
Spend about **45 minutes** on this Section.

Remember:
- Spend about 5 minutes planning and sequencing your material
- Write at least 1½ sides
- Spend about 5 minutes checking
    - ✓ your paragraphing   ✓ your punctuation   ✓ your spelling.

Either

3 A group of students from another country is coming to visit your school.
Write a letter welcoming them and **informing** them about:
- how to prepare for their visit
- what to expect on their visit
- the kinds of things they should look out for.

Start your letter with: Dear Students,

Or

4 Think about a difficult choice you have had to make. **Explain** what the choice
was, how you made it and what the consequences were.

Or

5 **Describe** a journey you have made. It could be a short journey, for example to
school, or a long journey, for example to a distant country.

Describe the journey so that your reader can picture it clearly.

Or

6 How many people have strong views on a topic such as cruelty to animals,
dangerous sports or environmental issues. Choose a topic you feel strongly
about. **Inform** your reader about it and **explain** your feelings and your reasons
for them.

ACKNOWLEDGEMENTS

The author and publishers would like to thank the following for permission to reproduce the following copyright material.

The publishers have made every effort to trace the copyright holders, but if they have inadvertently overlooked any, they will be pleased to make the necessary arrangements at the first opportunity.

Express Newspapers Syndications for the articles 'Air guns must be banned' 25 January, 2002, p12, 'Should cannabis now be legalised?' by Simon Hinde and John Triggs, 24 October, 2001, pp18-19, 'The school system that gives girls an advantage' p22, 'Why Asians don't want to corner the market in shops any more' 16 January, 2002 on pp167, 171, and the headline 'United's double act shatters sorry Spurs' 7 March, 2002, p28 from the *Daily Express*; Atlantic Syndications, on behalf of the *Daily Mail* for the article 'Would you believe it?' by Ivan Speck, 2 March, 2002 p15, and the headline 'I thought we would never get out alive' 20 November, 1996, p28 from the *Daily Mail*; Alberto Culver UK for their kind permission to reproduce the 'VO5 Select' advertisement and logo on p13; Glaxo Smith Kleine for the 'Oxy Pads' advertisement designed by Ogilvy & Mather on p25; the temperature map, thermometer and hours of dark on p27 are taken from the weather section of *The Times*, Wednesday March 6, 2002. Information supplied by the Met Office © Crown Copyright; the extract on p35 from article '"Great and Good" Have Blood on their Hands' is from p8 the *Sun*, Saturday, March 9, 2002, and the caption 'Roy Keane leapfrogs above his United colleague David Beckham in the pay stakes, but Beckham could soon overtake him' on p26 from *The Times* is © News International Newspapers Limited; Health Promotion England for 'Drugs & Sport' p28; D C Thomson & Co Ltd for the headline on p28 'Who will trust the spin doctors now' from the *Sunday Post*, 27 January, 2002, © D C Thomson & Co Ltd; Ackrill Media Group for the article on p31 'Jilted lover wrapped up like a mummy' from the *Northallerton, Thirsk and Bedale Times*; Wella UK for the Shaders & Toners' caption 'Dyeing for a boy-band binge on p28; *HarperCollins Publishers Limited* for the definition of 'fashion' on p36 from *Collins English Dictionary*, HarperCollins, 2000; The Watts Publishing Group Limited, 96 Leonard Street, London EC2A 4XD for the extract on p37 from *Timelines: Clothes*, Franklin Watts, 1992; Faber and Faber Limited for the extract on p39 from 'The Lady in the Van' from *Writing Home* by Alan Bennett; Independent Syndications for the article on p38 'Dilemma' by Virginia Ironside, from the *Independent*, 24 August, 1995; the *Guardian* for the article on p43 'Sliding Dior Galliano mixes his styles' by Jess Cartner-Morley, 21 January, 2002; The Random House Group Limited for the extract on p51 from *Touching The Void* by Joe Simpson, Jonathan Cape/Vintage; Plan International UK have kindly given permission to use extracts from their 'Sponsoring a child' leaflet on pp56-7, 62-3; Macmillan for the extracts from *Is That It?* by Bob Geldoff, on pp55, 61; the *Guardian* for the extract on p69 from 'The two-minute Guardian' 12 February, 2002; 'Lasting Bond' from TV Magazine, the *Sun*, 9-15 March, 2002 reproduced on p69 is © News International Newspapers Limited; the Orient Express luggage lables on p69 were used with the kind permission of Venice-Simplon-Orient-Express Limited; 'Humpty Goes Splatt!' on p69 is reproduced with the kind permission of Tutti-Frutti; Scholastic Limited for the extract on p71 from *Horrible Histories: Cruel Kings and Mean Queens* by Terry Deary, Scholastic; York College for the extract from their York College Prospectus on pp72-3; Warner Marketing for the text on Corton p75 from

Warner Brochure; Club 18-30 for the Bodrum Gumbet extract on p75 from their Summer 2002 brochure; *The Journal* for the letter on p77 'Fur coat's high price' by E D Irving; *Cycling & Mountain Biking Today* for the article 'The Bells, The Bells!' by Roger St Pierre on pp82-3; Egyptian Tourist Authority for 'Feluccas at Dawn' on p86; UNICEF UK for the 'Goma Volcano Children's Appeal' on p88; Proximity London, and WWF for the WWF toxic chemicals poster on p90; pp92-93 President Bush's Address to the Nation following attacks on the World Trade Centre and the Pentagon, September 11, 2001; EMAP for the letters 'Net Natter' on p96 and 'Telephone Tabs' on p97, from *Bliss*, July 2001; Rodale UK for the letters 'Getting an earful' on p97 and 'Nail Banging' on p98 from 'Ask Men's Health' from *Men's Health*, March 2002; extracts from the www.mindbodysoul.gov.uk website on pp100-101 © Crown Copyright; Amy Sohanpaul for the extract 'The safari traveller' on pp103-4 from *The Traveller's Handbook* by Jonathan Lorie and Amy Sohanpaul, WEXAS; Niyi Osundare has kindly given permission to reproduce on p114 an exract from his poem 'Not My Business'; Tom Leonard has kindly given his permission to reproduce on p114 an extract from his poem 'Unrelated Incidents no 3'; Bloodaxe Books for the extract on p114 from Moniza Alvi's poem 'Presents from my Aunts in Pakistan' published in *Carrying My Wife*, Bloodaxe Books, 2000; OUP India for permission to reprint the extract on p114 from 'Night of the Scorpion' by Nissim Ezekiel, from *Poverty Poems*, OUP India; New Directions Publishing Corp. for permission to reprint on pp116-17 'Two Scavengers in a Truck, Two Beautiful People in a Mercedes' by Lawrence Ferlinghetti, from *These Are My Rivers* © 1979 by Lawrence Ferlinghetti; Caroline Sheldon Literary Agency on behalf of John Agard for permission to reproduce on p125 the poem 'Half Caste' by John Agard, from *Get Back Pimple*, Penguin, 1996; Apa Publications for the extract on p139 from *Insight Guide: Caribbean*, Apa Publications 1992. All rights reserved; Time Warner Books UK for the extract on pp142-3 from *I Know Why the Caged Bird Sings* by Maya Angelou; OUP for the article on pp147-148 'Lean Lesson' by Matthew Bridgeman, from 'Sport' edited by John Foster, OUP; The Random House Group Limited for the extract on pp151-2 from *The Boys Are Back In Town* by Simon Carr, published by Arrow, and also for the extract on p154 from *To Kill A Mockingbird* by Harper Lee, published by William Heinemann; David Higham Associates Limited for the extract on p156 from *Going Solo* by Roald Dahl, Jonathan Cape and Penguin Books Limited; Carlton Books Limited for the extract on pp158-9 from 'The Enchanted Alley' by Michael Anthony, first published in *Cricket in The Road*, Andre Deutsch, 1973; The Women's Press for 'A Letter to My Brother' on p166 from 'Telling it like it is' from Livewire; the extract on p170 'When you don't feel like a foreigner' by Rita from *Community Writing* by Don Schiach, Nelson is reproduced by permission of the author.

The publishers would like to thank the following for permission to reproduce photographs on the pages noted:

SPL p10; AP p15; Rex 19; Daily Express pp18, 19; Education Photos p22, p148; *The Times* p26; the *Guardian* p43; Herbert Ponting/Popperfoto p46; Corbis p47, p139, pp167, 170 (Talvin Singh); Vintage Publishing p51; SRG pp72, 73; Collections/Alain Le Garsmeur p75 (top); Robert Harding p75 (bottom), p86 (top and bottom), 116, 125; Travel Ink p86 (middle); Associated Press pp92, 93; NHPA pp103, 104; Format p113; Arcaid p117; Scope pp167, 170 (Meera Syal, Ruby Hammer); Camera Press pp167, 170 (Michael Nasir); Empics pp167, 170 (Michael Chopra).